Early American

FURNITURE

You Can Build

By Ralph Treves

ARCO Publishing Company, Inc.

New York

Published by ARCO PUBLISHING COMPANY, INC.
219 Park Avenue South, New York, N.Y. 10003

Fifth Printing, 1976

Library of Congress Cataloging in Publication Data

Treves, Ralph.
  Early American furniture you can build.

  1. Furniture, American.   2. Furniture making—Amateurs'
manuals. I. Title.
TT195.T73   1976   684-1'042'0973   76-5410

ISBN 0-668-01215-3 (Library Edition)
ISBN 0-668-04004-1 (Paper Edition)

Printed in the United States of America

Photographs, where not otherwise credited, are by
Harold Siegfried.

CONTENTS

Photo courtesy of Old Sturbridge Village, Sturbridge, Mass

Reproducing Early
American Furniture

This furniture is prized for its rich color and rugged simplicity

Original furnishings of a tavern game-room emphasizes the spaciousness and uncluttered look of the early 18th century. Note wide wainscoting on the walls, iron door hinges and typical fireplace mantel.

Photos courtesy of Old Sturbridge Village, Sturbridge, Mass.

AUTHENTIC Early American originals are indeed hard to come by. The families that have retained some of the furniture through the generations cling to them as priceless heirlooms, and any items that sometimes become available are snapped up by museums, antique dealers and private collectors with unlimited funds.

Average individuals, particularly those who only lately have come to recognize the warmth, beauty and practical service of simple country-style furniture, can do quite well for themselves by taking their pick of the astounding range of excellent period reproductions and adaptations, some

at very moderate prices. You could also buy perfect replicas, custom-made by highly skilled craftsmen, if you don't have to worry about the price tag and the extra charge for putting in a few "time-worn" dents and scratches.

But you will get even more satisfaction, and at practically no cost, by making your own reproductions—modifying and adapting them to suit your own taste and needs so they will be, in fact, your own creations.

There is an appealing quality about Early American furniture. It is now prized more than ever as home furnishings because of its rich color and rugged simplicity that adapts so well to modern needs. Many of the finest new homes are built around the basic Early American decorative scheme. What is more, there's no need to take a rigid approach to the "antique" label and to make a fetish of exact duplication. It's the form that counts! So we make the most liberal use of the fundamental themes and apply them to our present-day world.

Early American isn't a "period" style, or the design of a few famed craftsmen, or the whimsey of a sovereign ruler. Rather, it is a *living* concept which grew out of the everyday needs and problems of the country folk in a new world. Thus, it is constantly adapted to circumstances far from the original purposes. In that way, you make your own original creations, the way you want them, and with your own hands. In time, these also may become precious to succeeding generations and even rate as "antiques" of the future.

Early American projects are particularly suited to the leisure-time hobbyist, even those who never before had attempted any sort of woodworking. It is possible for a complete novice to make several of the simpler projects, for instance, a little spice rack to hang above the stove. Whether you must work on the kitchen table, or are fortunate to have a nicely equipped workshop, the range of projects depends only on the skill you develop with experience, and the amount of time you wish to spend.

Some projects can be done with just a few hand tools such as a coping saw and a hammer; others require a rasp, plane, brace and bit, spokeshave, carpenter's saw, nailset, screwdriver, etc. Among power tools, one of the best for this hobby is a small electric saber saw, similar to a jig saw except that it is portable. It is highly efficient, versatile, and safe to use. And the proud owner of a more complete workshop containing a circular bench saw, lathe, drill press, and sander, is way ahead of the game. He should be able to tackle the most advanced projects given here, like the dry sink, wedge table, and sideboard with panel doors.

In this Old Sturbridge Village restoration, Sturbridge, Mass., the country home fireplace has a large, open hearth with brick paving. The rugged iron swing arm holds an immense kettle for hot water.

The wood used is of the lowest cost— usually good solid pine boards with knots and other blemishes which keep down the price. You can even use old wood—some enthusiastic hobbyists scour the countryside for planks and sidings from old, abandoned barns and sheds for this purpose. Odd pieces of scrap lumber, usually wasted because they cannot be worked with power tools, are quite suitable for many of the projects in this book.

In some projects, wood from old apple boxes is ideal, and in fact may be your best source for the thin ¼-inch stock that is sometimes needed.

Small, easy-to-handle pieces will do fine, in contrast to the cumbersome plywood panels used for making modern furniture. Assembly of Early American items is of the simplest kind—no need to be ashamed of plain butt joints, exposed end-grain, and even nail holes.

A separate chapter will guide you in selecting the wood for your projects, explain the technical designations and sizes, help you save money in your purchases by understanding the various grades and classifications, and describe the different species which are so generally considered to be just "pine" lumber.

Wherever possible, the text will list the amount of wood stock required for each project, and will also list other necessary supplies so you can estimate in advance the total cost of materials.

The lines of these furniture pieces are so basic and honest that they won't be marred by surface damage to the wood. Actually, such blemishes as dents, gouges, even splits, often add to their charm. (Cabinetmakers deliberately put them in to get that antique flavor.)

Pine is such a wonderful wood that it glows with any finish, acquires a desirable patina with age. It can be polished to an amazing gloss, or be kept in a subdued satiny finish. While considered a "soft" wood, pine is just as hard as some types of mahogany. Surface finishing, the part that stumps most home cabinet builders, is not difficult, though a really good finish takes some painstaking effort. Here again, pine shows its versatility in responding nicely to various oil stains, glazes, and a little hand rubbing.

The projects included in this book are all of the "country" or "farm" style, and the term Early American refers to the homely, hand-crafted products of the farmers who settled in outlying villages of New England, New York, New Jersey, Pennsylvania, Virginia and the Carolinas. Unable to carry heavy burdens of household goods, they had to make their own furniture from the native material available. But their handiwork retained some of the forms known to them in their past surroundings, mostly in England and Holland. Thus, there is a remarkable similarity in furniture from widely scattered sections,

Large kitchen of a home in Old Sturbridge Village has a harvest table with drop leaves, utensil cupboard, authentic peg rack on wall above stone tub and plank floors that have a well-scrubbed look.

such as the hutch cabinets, dower chests, trestle tables, cradles and pew benches.

The Early American designation often is incorrectly taken to mean "Colonial" furniture which was brought over from Europe by the boatload to fill the stately mansions that were built in the commercial and government centers of Boston, Philadelphia, Williamsburg, and Charlestown. Later, famed cabinetmakers such as Sheraton, Chippendale and others began producing this fine and intricate furniture in the colonies, shipping their products far and wide. This furniture, influenced by the elegance of the French and British courts, was followed by the more sedate "Federal" period during the first decades of the Republic, about the same time as the Empire designs which grew out of the Napoleonic era.

Within the Early American "country" categories there are various segments such as the Shakers, which is severely ascetic yet so glowingly beautiful; the Pennsylvania-Dutch and Pennsylvania-German, with their stylized decorations in the tulip-and-star motifs; the Quaker, Amish, Pilgrim and Puritan groupings, which fascinate the collector and art experts. You may find it extremely interesting and educational to delve further into the history and characteristics of this furniture which is so much a part of our country's heritage. Many fine exhibits like those of Old Sturbridge Village in Massachusetts, and

colonial Williamsburg in Virginia, are open to the public. Don't miss a visit to Paul Revere's home in Boston, Betsy Ross' home in Philadelphia, and other shrines kept in their original condition.

Some articles we use today as furniture were originally made as work tools. The cobbler's and saddler's benches now serve as cocktail tables in a multitude of forms, with variations in contour, superstructure, shelves and drawers. The kitchen dough box is perfect as a knitting chest, and even is found in thousands of homes as a magazine rack. The spinning wheel is a particular favorite and cannot be excelled for grace and beauty.

We go even further, by designing many present-day items with the Early American flavor. Knotty pine wall paneling is perhaps the most popular of all today. Kitchens have the Early American "look," achieved with down-to-earth pine cabinets. Dining rooms, dens and bedrooms are also styled for Early American decoration. Just recently, the national magazines carried advertisements for an "Early American air conditioner cover"! That brings history up to date!

So the emphasis here is not on ancient remnants, slick design, tricky hardware, and fancy joinery. What counts are usefulness, good proportions, tasteful outlines, bright finishings, and identification with our past traditions. All you have to do is to please yourself. •

Visitors watch in fascination as skilled craftsman at Old Sturbridge Village makes furniture reproductions in an original workshop, using only antique tools; above he is using a hand-turned wood lathe.

Choosing Tools and Woods

Pine is plentiful and economical, and projects require only simple tools

THE SATISFACTION and sense of achievement in making small furniture articles from wood are complemented by the fun of just working with hand tools. That is why some of the most prominent men in American life—statesmen, doctors, legislators, businessmen, actors and many others—consider woodworking their most relaxing and beneficial hobby, and take great pride in the skills they develop.

One fortunate characteristic of Early American furniture is that the work does not call for the precision required by modern furniture projects, thus more simple hand tools will do the job. Cabinet edges need not be perfectly square; in fact a little irregularity is desirable. There is little mitering and even then there is a good deal of difference between mitering the thin surface veneer of plywood, and jointing the solid edges of pine boards. Edges of frames are crudely rounded with a spoke-shave for that "country" look, instead of sleek uniform chamfering.

The Early American projects shown in this book cover a wide range, from the most simple to quite advanced workmanship. Some of them can be made with just two or three tools—a hammer, coping saw, and plane. Others may require additional tools such as a chisel, brace and bit, backsaw, gauges, etc.

As you acquire greater skill in woodworking, you will find it advantageous to build up your collection of tools until you have a fairly complete workshop. The outlay is very little, they will last a lifetime, and they will repay their cost many times over because good tools serve you over and over again.

The emphasis here is essentially on inexpensive hand tools to reproduce some of our colonial furniture designs just as they were made about two centuries ago. But don't overlook the benefits of having a few modern power tools. The most common electric tool is the drill; some brands of fairly good quality now can be bought for as little as $10, though better models run up to about $75. In recent years, the electric saber or "bayonet" saw has become extremely popular, is highly practical, and is used constantly for many jobs around the home. It is quite safe, can be used by anyone without any previous experience or training. These small hand saws cost from $25 to $95 for home models.

The Tools You Need

The essential tools for working with soft pine for these early American projects are: coping saw, claw hammer, ruler, combination square, block plane, rasp, nailset, screwdriver, brace and bit, carpenter's saw.

The following hand tools, purchased as needed for various projects, enable you to do better work, more easily and more quickly: surform plane and files, tape rule, expansive bits or circle saws, countersink bit, level, spokeshave, chisels, miter box, gluing clamps, marking gauge, doweling jig and plumb bob.

Recommended electric tools for the small home workshop are: electric drill, saber saw, oscillating sander, bench saw and woodturning lathe.

Selecting Your Tools

Coping saws are very inexpensive, running from as low as 50 cents to about $2. The size is based on the "throat" opening—the distance between blade and frame permitting clearance for cutting into a board. A saw with 6" to 7" clearance is preferred, with blades 6½" long.

The better saws are adjustable for angle cuts by twisting the blade holders. Blades cost 10 to 15 cents each, in various types and tool count for use in wood, plastics, plywood, etc.

Hammers. Claw hammers average $3 to $4 for excellent quality, including forged steel head and dependable hickory handle. Head weight usually is 16 ounces, but you may want also a lighter 10-ounce hammer for work with small nails and brads. The

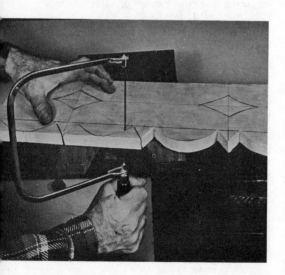

One of most frequently used tools is coping saw. Blade turns for curves or to reach into corners.

Combination square has center finder for circles and also comes with spirit level and protractor.

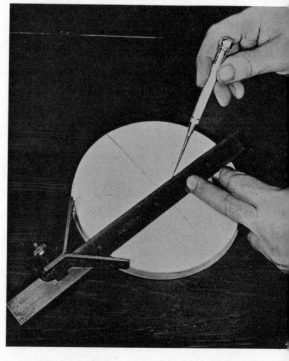

There are dozens of circle cutter bits. Shown is an expansion bit that makes holes up to 1½ inches.

Marking gauge makes guide lines for hand sawing; gives uniform spacings where desired on wood.

new tubular, rubber-coated handles with integrally locked claw head make an excellent tool.

Rulers. The zig-zag 6-foot rule is a "must" for every home and workshop. Get the "extension" type with a sliding brass bar at one end for internal measurements. Also, make sure the numbers are easy to read, printed on both sides of the rule, and of the type that won't rub off. Calibrations should be in 16ths of an inch. Prices for folding rules run about $2 to $3. A steel tape in 8- or 10-foot length is very handy. The new Stanley "Powerlock" tape has a device to lock the tape at the measured distance. You'll find this invaluable as it prevents errors in copying measurements. The tape case also has a spring clip so it can be carried in the belt to save wear on your pants pockets. Calibrations are printed on the polyester-film coating in yellow for easy reading. Price listed from $1.59 up.

Squares. These are vital to test the accuracy of your work. The ordinary try square is used for marking guide lines for cross-cutting boards with a hand saw, and for testing the edges of pieces to be joined. The combination square includes a sliding beam with spirit level, a turret protractor, and a centering head which enables you to instantly find the center of circles, draw accurate radius lines, etc.

Planes. A small block plane is used on almost every project for trimming and fitting parts. Larger planes, up to 9″ length, help smooth and square off boards. The new 4-edge cutter blades (Sears Roebuck) has disposable blades with cutting edge on each side, so there's no need for sharpening. Replacement blades cost less than $1. A very useful addition to your tool collection will be the Stanley Surform planes and files with thousands of tiny cutters which are excellent for trimming and smoothing end grain, and almost any kind of shaping or planing on wood.

Nailsets. For driving nail heads below the wood surface, a simple tempered steel punch is used in various sizes from $\frac{1}{32}$″ to ⅛″. Price only about 35 cents each. You also will want a needle-sharp scratch awl for locating screws and many other purposes.

Screwdrivers. Use the right size screwdriver for each type of screw to get cleaner work, more power in driving the screws, and to avoid marring the screw slots. Three or four different screwdrivers will be adequate for most work.

Amazing new tool is Stanley's Surform which acts as a plane to pare down wood or to smooth surface.

Miter box and backsaw combination is a real asset in workshop; saw is used for precision angle cuts.

Brace and bits. A brace with a fairly heavy frame makes the work easier, gives better torque for drilling and for driving larger screws all the way. A brace in the $5 price range will be adequate for average purposes. Auger bits cost from 75 cents to about $1.50 each depending on size. Also, get a countersink and screwdriver bit. An expansive bit also will be useful for cutting larger holes.

Saws. One of the greatest buys for your money is a good carpenter saw: taper-ground blade of the most perfect saw steel, heat-treated, hardened, tempered, and polished to a beautiful finish, teeth accurately set, and with a fine wood or plastic handle, perfectly balanced—all this at less than $5 for a tool that will give a lifetime of perfect service! Get either cross-cut or rip saw, or both, in 26-inch length for average use. You also can use a small dovetail saw with rigid bracing across the top for fine work. A backsaw 16" long is used in a miter box.

Other tools. While there's no point to just accumulating a vast storehouse of different tools, some of which will hardly ever be used, it's well worth while to get a few versatile items that come in handy, time and again, for better workmanship and wider range of projects.

A pair of sawhorses can be invaluable if you lack a good-size workbench. New Stanley sawhorse brackets (No. 362A) can

be disassembled in seconds and the parts stored flat in a corner when not needed. A set of chisels in various sizes, from ¼" to 1", is basic for any home workshop. A good metal miterbox, which can be set for bevel and angle cutting at any position, will repay its cost many times over. Others are a utility knife, plumb bob, large spirit level. An assortment of bar or pipe clamps can be used for regluing chairs, benches and other furniture that may become "rocky" after long use.

All of these items are quite low in cost, can be purchased one at a time as needed. A point that must be stressed is that the selection of each tool should be made with an eye to quality which will assure accuracy, safety in use, and long service.

Selecting the Wood

The early settlers of this country found pine lumber plentiful, readily available, and easy to work—and you will, too. The many species of pine are sold at every lumberyard, in every locality, and still are about the lowest cost wood you can buy.

For many of these projects, however, you won't have to buy any lumber at all because various scrap pieces of shelving boards can be used. That's part of the fun—making use of wood that would otherwise be thrown away, to produce a beautiful hutch cabinet or other pieces of furniture. Even wood with knots and streaks and wild grain will do, enhancing the rustic "country" appearance of the furniture.

However, for some projects you will need larger stock, and may even want "matched" boards with similar characteristics, such as color, graining and knots.

For most regular projects, the preferred wood is Ponderosa pine, soft-textured wood with close, uniform grain, easily sanded to a smooth surface, and most important, is excellent to work with. The color is distinctly light, ranging from creamy white to straw. Shrinkage is moderate, about the same as other light-weight woods, while nailing properties are excellent because of resistance to splitting. Ponderosa pine responds well to finishes, will take penetrating stain deeply and uniformly, while the surface can be polished to a beautiful, glowing patina.

Ponderosa pine is available in thicknesses from $\frac{5}{8}''$ to 2", which when dressed becomes $\frac{9}{16}''$ for the $\frac{5}{8}''$ size, and 25/32" for the 1" size. Board widths come up to 12". It is better to buy the narrower widths if they serve your purpose, as the 12-inch stock tends to warp or become bowed at the center.

Your single problem will be to find a source for $\frac{1}{4}''$-thick solid pine stock. This thickness is not generally carried by local lumber dealers, though some will order it for you from the mill. You probably can get all you want from any wood box factory in your locality, though the fact is that there are fewer box makers than ever because of the widespread use of corrugated cartons.

However, there still are plenty of wood crates and boxes around, and a single box will provide enough of the $\frac{1}{4}''$ wood for several small projects. Don't worry if the wood seems to be very coarse and rough, as it will take very little effort to sand it smooth. Thus, you can get the $\frac{1}{4}''$ stock free by just a little effort, perhaps by asking your grocer or vegetable dealer to save a couple of boxes for you, or by checking around at some plants or offices in your community that receive shipments.

If you want selected fine wood, of any specifications, a good source is one of the national wood supply firms like Albert Constantine and Son, Inc., of 2050 Eastchester Road, New York 61, N. Y., which carries a tremendous stock of select, milled lumber of any type and species, and will ship your order according to your specifications. Also, at Constantines, you can obtain any special hardware for Early American projects like black iron drawer pulls,

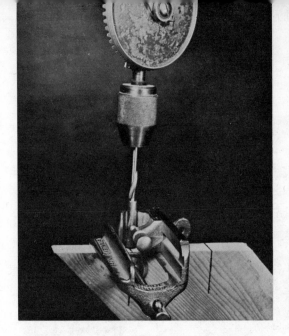

Dowel jig is a device that automatically aligns holes for jointing and other dowel assemblies.

door hinges and latches, and the Lazy Susan turntable for the table project included in this book. This firm sells the various stains needed for finishing the projects, and a full stock of various hand tools. A catalogue listing the lumber, tools, hardware and accessories can be obtained for 25 cents.

In at least one project—the built-in knotty pine wall cabinet which covers up a former doorway, you will need tongue-and-groove knotty pine boards to make the back wall paneling. For this project, the best lumber to use is Idaho white pine with a few very small knots. Idaho pine has excellent dimensional stability, smoothness of surface, attractive even-textured graining. The wood is light in color, varying from nearly white to a pale reddish brown, and is easily finished with paint or stain. One of its most important properties is its ability to take nails without splitting. Thus, it can be "blind nailed" through the thin tongue between each board for a very neat installation.

Another choice paneling wood is sugar pine, in either knotted or clear grades. Its color is creamy white which darkens as it ages to a pale brown, sometimes tinged with pink. Both woods are graded as select, common and factory. The select grade is divided into three classifications: supreme, choice and quality. The common is usually sold as either common No. 1, or better "common" which is really No. 2 common. For paneling, use regular one-inch thickness. •

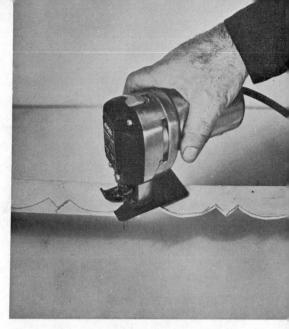

A jig saw makes inside or outside cuts, to any shape, can do intricate and precise scroll work.

Electric saber saw is one of the most effective portables, easy to use even by the inexperienced.

The small, lightweight oscillating sander helps to smooth the surface and make it ready for finishing.

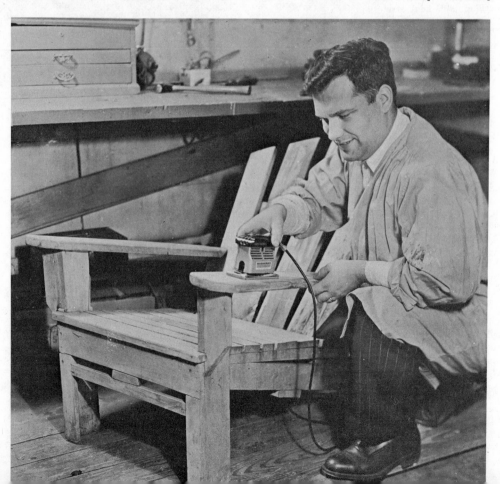

Wood Finishing

Quality of finish will depend on the amount of care and effort you expend

Prepare the cabinet for finishing with final sanding, using 3/0 paper, and wipe off all sanding dust.

PINE lends itself to finishing with fewer problems than most other woods. Many connoisseurs regard pine as superior because of its richness and depth of color, the smooth feel of the surface, its glowing patina. A unique aspect is that dents, gouges and knots that would be ruinous blemishes in furniture of other woods, actually add to the decorative values of pine.

Equipment needed for finishing includes a couple of good brushes, a few wads of cloth, some sandpaper and steel wool. The entire work can be done nicely by hand without great exertion, but it will be helpful, certainly, if you have a small electric sander (the oscillating type) and a power spray gun for applying successive coats of clear lacquer.

The materials include a small amount of oil stain of the desired color (either prepared stains or mix your own), some wood filler, pumice or rottenstone, and shellac,

clear varnish or lacquer for the finish coatings. Various commercial polishes and waxes will help get special effects. With certain woods, a bleaching agent is desirable to tone down "off" colors.

Early American furniture is stained, rather than painted, to retain the natural wood grain. Any type of stain or coloring material may be used, even shoe polish, to achieve interesting finishes.

The method emphasized in this book is done with oil stain, preferred because it is easiest to apply and will give highly satisfactory results. This stain consists of tung oil or linseed oil to which pigments are added to obtain the right color. The old-time raw umber, and raw or burnt sienna, are widely used, but better color control is possible with regular oil pigments purchased in small tubes. Transparent pigments are advised, rather than the opaque types which may cause a muddy appear-

Remove drawers and hardware. Fill all nail holes with filler tinted with pigment to match color.

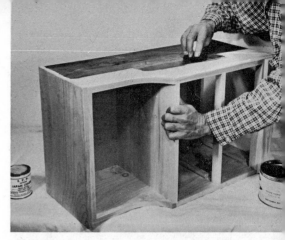

Mix the stain to the desired color and apply it with cloth pad along the sides and top of cabinet.

Hard-to-reach areas inside a cabinet are cleaned thoroughly and then stained with a small brush.

Drawers are done separately. Do just the front with stain. Shellac the balance for cleanliness.

ance. The oil stain is applied with a brush or cloth pad. If a brush is used, make sure that bristles are tight; twirl the brush to remove any loose bristles which will foul the work. No grain sealer is needed for pine, but a preliminary application of linseed oil may be used to control depth of absorption.

Acid, water, and alcohol stain finishes also are suitable but require considerable experience for correct application.

Instead of staining, you may prefer to keep the wood in its natural color with a few coatings of water-clear brushing lacquer which is practically colorless and won't discolor wood. White shellac, clear varnish, or penetrating wood sealer, buffed to a fine gloss, will serve the same purpose.

Some homeowners prefer a simple coating of hard wax, directly over the sanded raw wood, to retain the light, natural color. Chrome yellow or darker brown pigments may be used to tint the wax which is melted down and applied in liquid form, while still hot, for deeper penetration.

There are nine definite steps in finishing furniture, and in the following order:

1. Prepare the surface by sanding and cleaning the work thoroughly to form a sound base for a perfect finish. Start with No. 1 garnet paper to remove any marks made by woodworking tools or machines. Round off the corners and edges, paying particular attention to the exposed end grain which should be sanded down as smooth as the surface stock. Finish up with

After stain is wiped and has dried, put on wash coat of thin shellac and allow to dry thoroughly.

The shellac coat is rubbed with fine steel wool, followed with 6/0 sandpaper or pumice in water.

3/0 paper, for the final sanding, after wiping the wood with a damp cloth to raise any loose fibers. Holes usually are filled after the stain coat, using a prepared wood filler or Spackle compound. Since the filler will not take the stain, it should be tinted with pigment to match the color as closely as possible.

Remove drawer knobs, hardware, take out the drawers to be finished separately. Brush out any wood dust.

2. Mix the penetrating oil stain, using oil soluble powder stains or regular oil colors in tubes. Pine finishes tend to darken in time, due to chemical change of the surface wood, so a somewhat lighter shade than ultimately desired should be used. Light browns, reddish browns, tans, beige, honey brown, "maple" and black oak colors are most favored.

Make frequent tests on scrap pieces of the same wood until you have the color you like best. Remember that woods vary in tone, density and color, which will make a difference in the final appearance.

If your wood is too dark or has a tint that makes it difficult to match the finish with another piece of furniture, you can bleach the wood with oxalic acid crystals dissolved in boiling water to make a concentrated solution. Apply while hot, with a brush, and allow to dry. Remove any whitish "bloom" with alcohol that may show up, then sand smooth. *Caution:* oxalic acid is highly poisonous and should be

handled with care. Discard any leftover. Various commercial bleaches also are effective for wood treatment, such as Clorox, Purex, etc.

3. Apply oil stain with a cotton pad, or brush. Cover every part, except inside the drawers, with direct applications of the stain. Don't allow the stain to "run" in rivulets down the sides as this may result in streaking because of longer penetration of those parts. End grain is handled more carefully, just a small amount of stain is put on and immediately wiped off to prevent excessive darkening.

When the entire area is covered, allow to penetrate for about 5 minutes, then wipe off, while still wet, with a cloth.

4. At this time, fill all the nail holes with tinted wood filler or yellow beeswax. Also, before the final finishing coats go on, this is your chance to bring out some interesting highlights in the cabinet by lightly sanding certain knots or prominent grain. This lightens the color somewhat in relation to the rest of the piece. On the other hand, certain spots or graining may require additional applications of stain for blending.

5. After the stain dries, apply a wash coat of shellac to prevent bleeding through of the stain color. Use a "thin" shellac, reduced with alcohol, 4 to 1. With a "4-pound cut" white shellac, add about one third to one half as much alcohol, which will brush on easier and smoother. The

Second and third shellac undercoats are applied, each coat rubbed with fine sandpaper, and dusted.

Final coat is rubbed with pumice and water, or oil, to bring up finish for waxing or polishing.

thinned shellac may also be used in a 50-50 mixture with brushing lacquer.

Apply the full wash coat to cover the entire area, allow to dry thoroughly (about 3 to 4 hours). There need be no concern about overlapping or streaking; just make sure to get complete coverage. The shellac brush will be very difficult to restore to original condition no matter how often it is rinsed in alcohol, so it is better to set aside a special brush for shellac and soften the bristles each time by soaking in alcohol for a couple of hours. Bristles may become curled or bent, but that will not matter.

6. Rubbing with fine 00 steel wool or No. 6/0 sandpaper after the wash coat smooths out the surface, removes bubbles and dust and prepares a good surface for the final coats. Rub only in the direction of the grain. Clean the surface thoroughly before applying the finish coats.

7. Finish coatings. At least three coats of thinned shellac, or two coats of varnish, or four coats of lacquer should be applied to bring up the color, give depth to the finish and provide a hard protective finish coating.

All undercoats of shellac are rubbed with 00 steel wool. Second and third coats of varnish are rubbed with 6/0 sandpaper in water; lacquer coatings are rubbed with lacquer rubbing compound. An electric oscillating sander may be used for undercoat rubbing, using a felt pad under the sandpaper for uniform contact. Orbital

sanders are not advisable for finish sanding because they tend to form circle markings.

8. Polishing. The final coat of shellac or varnish is polished with fine pumice in water, rubbed only in direction of the grain with a soft rubbing felt about 3"x5". Follow with rottenstone in water for a higher polish. Clean surface with benzine and allow to dry before applying any polishing oil.

For lacquer, use special rubbing compounds and lacquer polish in addition to the pumice and rottenstone, or sand with 8/0 paper lubricated with thin solvent oil, like benzine, on the final coat to get a high gloss.

9. Waxing. Applying the wax calls for the hardest physical exertion of the entire finishing project, if a proper gloss is to be obtained. Use a good quality wax containing a fair percentage of hard carnauba in mineral spirits, such as turpentine. Apply the wax with a cloth, spreading evenly over the surface and all small side parts.

A fairly thick application may be made at one time, though this will call for considerable rubbing. Use a soft cloth pad and rub on long strokes with the grain. For the ultimate in fine furniture finishing that will equal professional work, apply several thin coats of wax in series, each thoroughly polished. When finished, the hard wax will offer adequate protection; keep the furniture projects in good condition. •

Pin-Up Planter Lamp

This simple project will add light and beauty to any small room

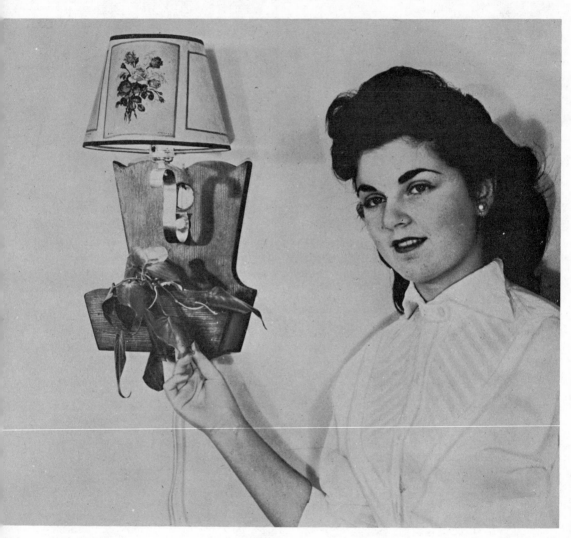

A COUPLE of scrap pieces of 1x10 shelving board will be sufficient to make one of these handsome pin-up planter lamps for a child's bedroom or the dinette. Occasional light from the lamp is sufficient to keep your plants thriving. Small knots in the board will enhance the "woody" appearance. Just make sure the parts are sanded very smooth and that the final staining is in a light color that won't obscure the graining.

The board for the back plaque is 9 inches wide, 10¾ inches long—the grain running lengthwise. The front is 3¾ by 9 inches—the grain running horizontally. An alternate design with slightly different dimensions is also shown in the drawings.

The first step is to draw your patterns on thin cardboard by following the outlines shown in the diagram, guided by a grid of one-inch squares drawn on the cardboard. Cut out the cardboard pattern and trace the outlines directly on the wood.

Drill the center hole in the plaque with

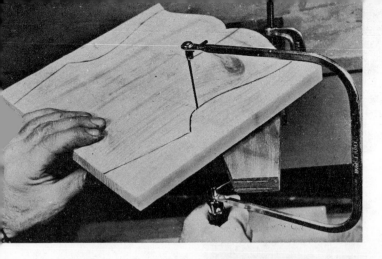

Graceful curves can be cut with a jig saw or coping saw. Finish edges with rasp and then sandpaper them smooth.

Left, illumination from even a low wattage bulb is enough to provide sustaining light for the foliage in the planter box.

Decorative hole in back of lamp is also used to hang the unit. An adjustable bit is used to drill the hole.

an expansion bit, and smooth the edges of both front and back with a file and sandpaper. If the sawing produced irregular spots, straighten them out the best you can with a rasp and sandpaper.

The bottom section is 2½ by 5 inches, cut from the same wood, the two sides are 2½ by 2½ inches, as shown in the drawing. The bottom is centered along the edge of the plaque and nailed from the back, then the front is nailed on, allowing equal clearance at both ends. Use 1½-inch finishing nails, and countersink the heads.

The top edge of each side is rounded with a plane, sandpaper, or cornering tool. Insert the sides at a slight outward flare between front and back, and nail them in to complete the woodworking part of the project.

Next comes the copper bracket, which is a strip 1 by 8 inches long. Brass or aluminum may be substituted. This is curved into an "S" shape by hammering it around a length of pipe or tubing having approxi-

Assemble parts with finishing nails. Countersink heads and fill holes with pigmented wood putty before finishing.

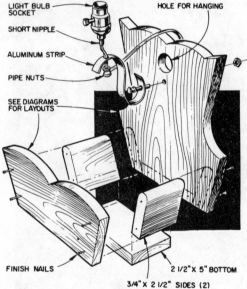

LIGHT BULB SOCKET

HOLE FOR HANGING

SHORT NIPPLE

ALUMINUM STRIP

PIPE NUTS

SEE DIAGRAMS FOR LAYOUTS

FINISH NAILS

2 1/2" X 5" BOTTOM

3/4" X 2 1/2" SIDES (2)

8½"

3⅝"

10¾"

1" SQUARES

2½"

¼"

2½"

5"

3¾"

9¼"

10¾"

ALTERNATE DESIGN AND BLANKS

3½"

mately a 2-inch outside diameter. Drill a ⅝-inch diameter hole at the arc of one curve, and a similar hole near the end of the opposite curve. If your drill will take only a ¼-inch bit, you can enlarge the holes to the required diameter with an ordinary pipe reamer, as the soft copper cuts easily. The copper can be burnished by rubbing with steel wool and scouring powder, then protected with a coat of lacquer.

The lamp parts consist of a socket of the type having the cord outlet on the side rather than at the bottom, and a 1½-inch length of threaded pipe nipple with two lock nuts. When the lamp socket is assem-

bled, the cord is arranged along the back of the copper bracket and is drawn through the nipple. The lock nuts on the nipple hold the bracket firmly.

A variation of the pin-up lamp has a simplified bracket and slightly different contours. The lamp bracket is made of a strip of ¾-inch-wide copper or brass, about 10 inches long. This is gently curved to the shape shown in the drawing and drilled 2 inches from one end for fastening to the back plaque with a ¼-inch bolt. The other end, flaring away from the back panel to extend about 6 inches from the wall, is drilled 1½ inches from the other end for the socket mounting. •

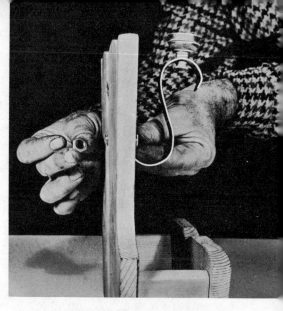

Make "S" curve bracket by hammering the 1x8-inch strip of copper around a 2-inch diameter pipe.

The metal lamp bracket is drilled for socket and the assembly is mounted on back board, as shown.

Alternate design of bracket for the lamp is shown below. Patterns for both are on opposite page.

Attractive spoon rack combines the gleam of your antique silver with the warm glow of polished pine.

Spoon Rack

A traditional piece brought to the New World from Europe

THE SPOON RACK was a traditional decoration during colonial days because of its Old World flavor. This is an interesting project, planned so it could be made entirely by hand with just a few small tools: a coping saw, backsaw, plane, hammer, brace and ¼-inch bit. The wood is ⅜-inch stock throughout.

First saw the back panel to 10- by 16-inch size. Make the two side notches at

the bottom of this panel $3\frac{3}{16}$ inches high and just the depth equal to the thickness of your stock, which may be slightly more or less than ⅜ inch. Next, cut out the scrollwork design at the top as shown in the drawings.

The two side pieces of the lower compartment can be made with a single diagonal cut across a board $3\frac{3}{16}$ inches wide and 9⅛ inches long. Mark the 5-inch

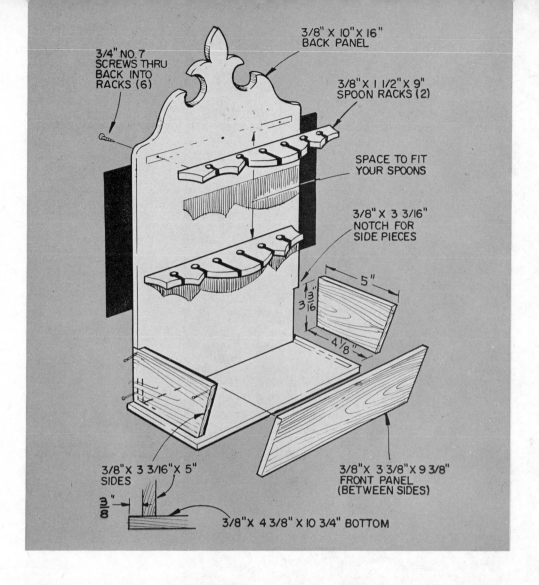

3/8" X 10" X 16" BACK PANEL

3/4" NO. 7 SCREWS THRU BACK INTO RACKS (6)

3/8" X 1 1/2" X 9" SPOON RACKS (2)

SPACE TO FIT YOUR SPOONS

3/8" X 3 3/16" NOTCH FOR SIDE PIECES

5"

3/16 3"

4 1/8"

3/8"X 3 3/16"X 5" SIDES

3/8 "

3/8"X 3 3/8"X 9 3/8" FRONT PANEL (BETWEEN SIDES)

3/8"X 4 3/8" X 10 3/4" BOTTOM

position on one narrow edge, then the 5-inch position on the opposite edge, measuring from the other end of the board. Draw the line across and make the cut to get the two sides.

Fit the two sides into their notches and attach with brads from the back. Cut the bottom board 4⅜ by 10¾ inches, center it so there is an equal overhang on both ends, and nail it on, from below, into the side pieces and the bottom edge of the back panel. The front is cut 3⅜ inches wide by 9⅜ inches long, and beveled slightly with a plane to fit into the angle formed by the sides. Attach this to complete the lower compartment.

Make the spoon holders from two strips 1½ inches wide by 9 inches long. Both strips can be shaped together so they will be uniform. Tack them together, temporarily. Drill a series of six holes with a ¼-inch bit, then shape the front as shown in the drawings. Cut the notches through to the circles. These notches should be made smaller than the holes so the spoons will stay in place. You may have to use a larger retainer hole if your antique spoons have exceptionally wide handles.

Both rails are attached to the back panel with several No. 6 or No. 7 screws. The best way to locate the screw positions so they will enter the holders is to set the holders in place and outline them with light pencil marks. Then with an awl, make thin holes through the board. The screws then can be driven through the back and will be in correct position. •

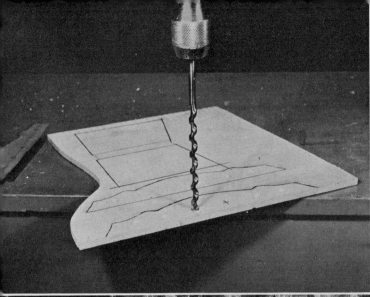

Lay out the parts directly on wood stock for cutting. Drill a row of holes with ¼-inch bit on holder bar.

Sides can be made with a single piece of stock by marking a diagonal that gives a proper end angle.

The bottom edge of front panel is beveled to conform to angle in which it rests against the sides.

The sides are set into the mortises cut into the back panel. Parts are nailed in using thin headless brads.

Narrow slots are cut into the spoon holder bar, making an opening into the holes drilled previously.

Curved outlines of back-board and holder bars are drawn on ½-inch squares and traced on wood stock.

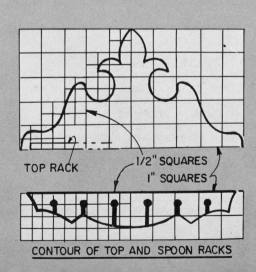

TOP RACK

1/2" SQUARES

1" SQUARES

CONTOUR OF TOP AND SPOON RACKS

25

Shaker Doll Cradle

Charmingly simple, this sentimental echo from the past is easily duplicated with hand tools

No Christmas gift will be more joyfully received than a hand-wrought cradle for her favorite doll.

YOU CAN DELIGHT any little girl by presenting her with this Early American doll cradle. If available, a circular saw can be used, but this project can be made with simple hand tools—a good hand saw, a coping saw, a hammer and screwdriver, plus a rasp and cornering tool for rounding the edges. The materials cost very little, too. You'll need an 8-foot length of ½-inch pine board, 12 inches wide, and a piece of 1-inch stock, 6 inches wide and about 15 inches long. Since a few tight knots will add to the appearance of the side boards and

reduce the cost at the same time, buy only No. 2 common grade wood.

The work proceeds in two stages: first comes the base consisting of rocker runners attached to the platform. Then the top section, with its characteristic hood, is assembled and mounted on the platform. The drawings show the dimensions and shape of each part.

Begin by laying out a grid of one-inch squares on kraft paper and trace the outlines of the sides, for which you have a full pattern, and the runners and canopy brace,

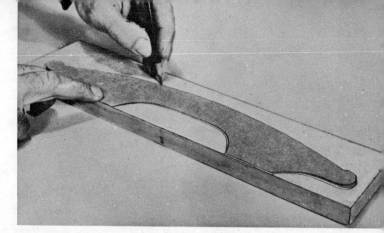

Using dimensions shown in the drawing on page 29 make paper templates for tracing.

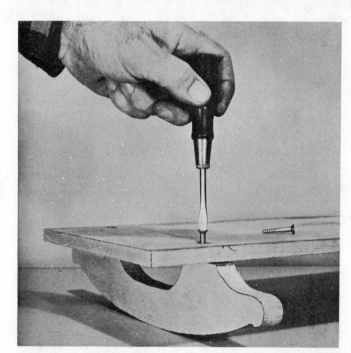

All parts are cut from half-inch thick wood except for the rockers which are 1" stock.

Head and foot panels have tapered sides. If these are cut on table saw use tapering jig.

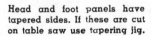

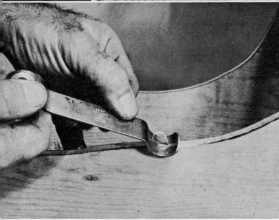

Nail sides to head and foot panels with brads as shown in photo, top left. Use glue if desired.

Canopy brace is attached to sides with screws. Support brace with wood scrap when nailing.

Cornering tool, left, quickly rounds off edges of wood after cutting, contributes antique look.

for which you have half patterns. Cut out the paper patterns and trace the outlines directly on the wood for sawing.

Cut the platform 8½x24 inches in size, round off the edges and corners. The two rockers are the only parts made of 1-inch stock, for which you'll need a piece about 15 inches long. Note that the rockers have turned ends which keep the cradle from tipping over when rocked too vigorously. They are shaped with a coping saw, or if available, a jig saw. The curved bottom edge should be smoothed neatly with the rasp. Attach each rocker 3 inches from each end of the platform, turning screws down through the platform. Make sure the rockers are placed uniformly so there is free movement of the platform.

The top cradle section is assembled next. Saw the two sides, about 27 inches long, then the head and foot panels—angled as shown in drawings. Follow guide lines drawn on the wood when cutting with a hand saw. On a circular saw, the angles for the panels are obtained by using an ad-

justable taper jig. Make sure the work is turned upside down for the second cut when using this jig so both angles will taper in the correct direction.

Join the sides to the panels with a series of finishing nails or thin brads through the sides. Then shape the canopy brace, which should have the same curve as the top of the head panel. Attach this brace with screws. The canopy is formed with 1-inch-wide strips, ten in number, placed closely together and nailed to both the curved brace and the top of the head panel. The top section now is complete and is joined to the platform with glue and small screws from the bottom.

All exposed edges, particularly along the sides, are rounded with the cornering tool which is a bent strip of hardened metal with a beveled slot that shaves off long slivers of the wood.

Before staining, the entire cradle should be carefully sanded, with close attention to the edges. Nailheads should be counterset and holes packed with putty. •

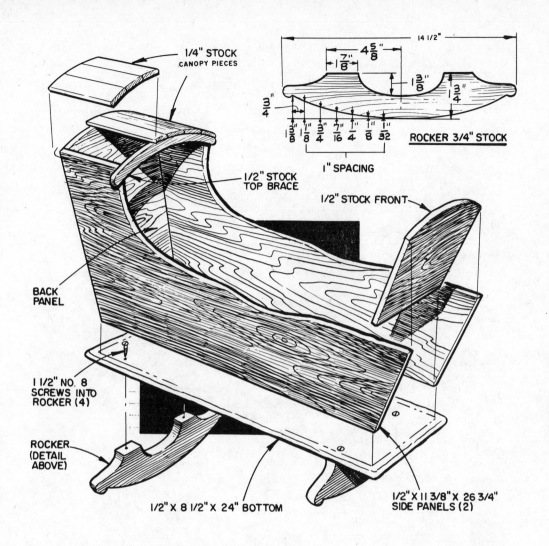

1/4" STOCK
CANOPY PIECES

14 1/2"

4 5/8"

7/8"

1 3/8"

1 3/4"

3/4"

ROCKER 3/4" STOCK

3/8" 1 1/8" 3/4" 7/16" 1/4" 1/8" 3/32"

1" SPACING

1/2" STOCK
TOP BRACE

1/2" STOCK FRONT

BACK
PANEL

1 1/2" NO. 8
SCREWS INTO
ROCKER (4)

ROCKER
(DETAIL
ABOVE)

1/2" X 8 1/2" X 24" BOTTOM

1/2" X 11 3/8" X 26 3/4"
SIDE PANELS (2)

Drawing, above, shows how pieces go together. Note that ½″ stock is used except for rockers and top.

Canopy top is made of thin strips of ¼″ wood, the two rockers are jig-sawed out of one-inch stock.

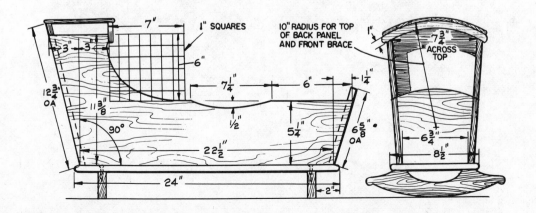

7"

1" SQUARES

10" RADIUS FOR TOP
OF BACK PANEL
AND FRONT BRACE

1"

7 3/4"
ACROSS
TOP

3" 3"

6"

12 3/4"
OA

11 3/8"

7 1/4"

6"

1/4"

1/2"

90°

5 1/4"

6 5/8"
OA

6 3/4"

22 1/2"

8 1/2"

24"

2"

Latticed Wall Rack

Grill of brass rods offers support to the framework
and adds grace and beauty to its appearance

Sides and top are shaped with a saber saw. Sides can be joined temporarily to cut them uniformly.

At left, crossed rods are interesting feature of the wall rack with group of drawers for small items.

Drill series of holes in each retainer block, two rows in each strip, to hold the brass rods in position.

IN WARM-LOOKING pine, and beautifully proportioned, this wall case features a distinctive lattice grill made of gleaming brass rod. Its two knickknack shelves are supplemented by eight small drawers, very handy for keeping odds and ends.

The case is made entirely of ¼-inch-thick solid pine stock, once so readily available merely by breaking up any fruit box but now more difficult to come by since all packing is done in corrugated cartons. Some lumber dealers carry this material in stock, but if that source fails, you can obtain the wood by mail order from one of the crafts supply firms.

The thin wood is easily worked to form the unit. First rip two pieces to 3¼-inch width and 20-inch length. In each of these sides, make four shallow dado grooves for shelves as indicated in the drawing. Tack the two sides together (grooved surfaces

face to face) and cut the curved outline with band saw or coping saw, as shown in the diagram.

Cut the ¼-inch back panel 16¼ inches wide by 9 inches deep. Rip the three upper shelves 3 inches wide and a length equal to the width of the back panel plus the depth of your dado cuts—which probably will come to a total of 16⅜ inches. The back panel extends down only to the top of the brass lattice.

Cut the scrollwork at the top of the back panel. Assemble the parts that are ready. The three shelves go into their dado grooves and are flush with the front edge of the sides. If necessary, make adjustments by ripping the back panel slightly. Glue and nail the shelves into place.

The lattice is made of brass rods, about ⅛ inch diameter. Cut two wood strips, 7/16 by 7/16 inch, to fit into the case between the sides. Drill a hole at each end,

Rods are easily bent in small metal block, drilled to a required depth to make sure of uniform bend.

Brass rods are assembled in retainer strips held together with tape until the section is fitted in rack.

Two shelves, when fitted into grooves cut into the side panels, will hold the latticed assembly in place.

32

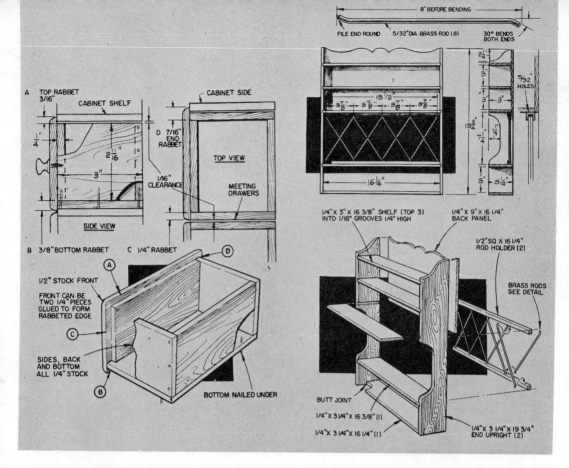

and a double row of three holes equally spaced along the strips.

The rods are bent slightly at the ends to form the lattice. The brass rods are dull-looking when you buy them but are easily brightened by rubbing with fine sand-paper. A coat of clear lacquer or shellac will keep them glistening.

Bending may be done in a vise, or on a block of steel in which a hole is drilled to receive the rod. Bend all the rods uniformly, then fit them between the two wood strips as shown. If necessary, hold the rod assembly together with masking tape until the grill can be placed into the shelf case.

The next shelf, which is ¼ inch deeper than the others because there is no back panel, is slipped into its grooves and holds the grill in place. The bottom shelf then is tacked in between the sides.

The unit may be used either as open shelves, or fitted with the group of eight small drawers as shown. These may be made of the same ¼-inch stock except for the drawer fronts, which will have to be ½ inch or more in thickness to hold the sides and bottom. A thorough sanding and ap-

plication of selected oil stain will make a fine finished piece. Brass knobs can be purchased or tiny drawer knobs can be made of ½-inch dowel.

Simplest way to make the drawers is by "doubling up" on the front stock, gluing a piece of ¼-inch stock to a larger piece of the same stock to form the drawer front. The outside part extends sufficiently beyond the drawer space to overlap half the thickness of the shelves above and below, and at one side for an end drawer. The inside part is small enough to allow a recess on all four sides so that the two drawer sides and bottom can be attached into the recess and still leave a little extra space for the outside overlap.

The get the dimensions right, it is best to assemble the inside drawer parts first (the sides, back and bottom) then add the extra front piece which is cut to the dimensions required. There are two different widths of drawers, but all are 3 inches deep, so the sides can all be cut at one time.

The front pieces are rounded along the edges and at the corners for attractive appearance. •

Farmer's Lantern

Electrified antique lamp is made of wood, fiberglass and metal

THE OLD-TIME farmer's lantern has considerable charm. In its modern, electrified version, it is practical for softly lighting a room corner, and is sure to serve as a "conversation piece" among folk handicraft buffs.

You may want a pair for yourself and while you're at it, make several others for novel gifts by duplicating the parts. Thin translucent plastic is used for the lamp sides; in color if you prefer.

Use ¼-inch or ⅜-inch-thick solid wood for the top and bottom plates, each 5½ inches square. A 1¼-inch hole is drilled at the center of one plate to receive the lamp socket. Four vent holes, ⅜ inch in diameter, also are drilled in this top plate, at least ½ inch away from the center hole so the wood won't split.

Rip eight pieces of solid stock, each 10 inches long, to ⅜- by ⅜-inch size. Four of these pieces will be used for the corner risers, so they must be grooved on two adjacent sides to receive the plastic shields.

The other pieces receive only a single groove in one side, and will be used for the top and bottom retainers.

The plastic shields are 4¼ by 8½ inches. It's better to have them on hand before you start so that grooves can be cut to fit their thickness. The plastic, usually of fiberglass, is easily cut with a saw.

The top and bottom plates are temporarily tacked together and a ⅜-inch hole drilled at each corner through both pieces about ¼ inch from each edge. Identify the corners with numbers so the holes can be matched later. With a narrow triangular file, or a chisel, square off these drilled holes so the ⅜- by ⅜-inch vertical strips can be pushed through.

Next, saw a thin slot into the top plate between two side posts, in line with their grooves, so one side panel can be lifted for access to the lamp bulb inside. Also, drill a tiny hole in all four posts, ½ inch from each end, for the little wood pegs that will lock the assembly together.

Caps for top and bottom of the lamp are cut from ¼-inch stock. Corner holes squared with file.

Holes are drilled in top piece for light socket and venting of heated air. Note slot in one side.

Photo on facing page shows the completed lamp. Unit is suspended from metal bracket firmly attached to the wall.

Picture at right shows the porcelain lamp socket and how it is unscrewed. The threaded metal part goes through hole.

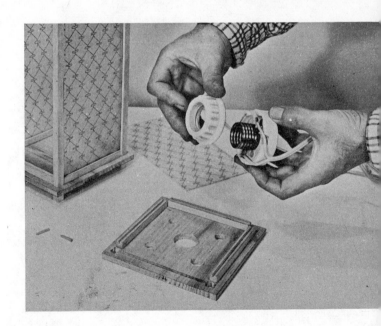

Place the four posts into the corner holes of the bottom plate and press the pegs into the holes underneath so the plate rests on the pegs. Cut the four remaining ⅜- by ⅜-inch strips into 4½-inch lengths to fit b e t w e e n the vertical members. (Check this dimension and adjust for a good fit.) These strips are glued and tacked with brads to the bottom plate between each corner post. Three of these strips also are fastened between the square holes to the top plate in the same way, but no

Assemble the parts as shown in the sketch and finish by inserting the small pegs as shown in the photo at right.

The fourth panel is removable so that burned-out bulbs may be easily replaced. Tubular bulb is recommended in lamp.

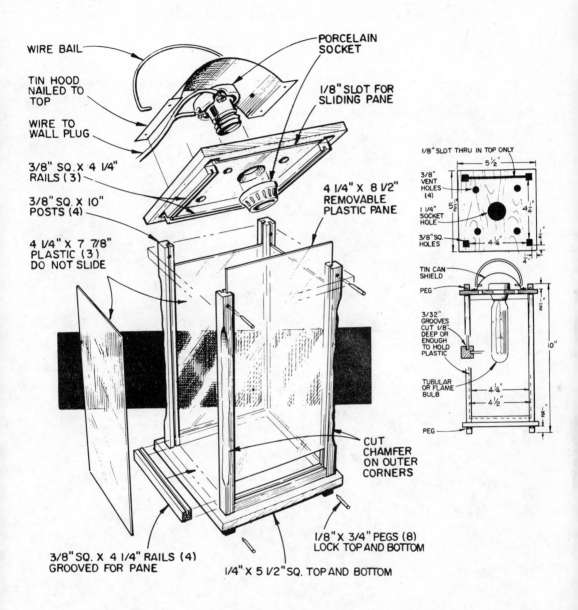

WIRE BAIL

TIN HOOD NAILED TO TOP

WIRE TO WALL PLUG

3/8" SQ. X 4 1/4" RAILS (3)

3/8" SQ. X 10" POSTS (4)

4 1/4" X 7 7/8" PLASTIC (3) DO NOT SLIDE

PORCELAIN SOCKET

1/8" SLOT FOR SLIDING PANE

4 1/4" X 8 1/2" REMOVABLE PLASTIC PANE

1/8" SLOT THRU IN TOP ONLY

5 1/2"

3/8" VENT HOLES (4)

5 1/2"

1 1/4" SOCKET HOLE

4 1/4"

3/8" SQ. HOLES

4 1/4"

1/4"

TIN CAN SHIELD

PEG

3/32" GROOVES CUT 1/8" DEEP OR ENOUGH TO HOLD PLASTIC

TUBULAR OR FLAME BULB

PEG

4 1/4"

4 1/2"

10"

CUT CHAMFER ON OUTER CORNERS

3/8" SQ. X 4 1/4" RAILS (4) GROOVED FOR PANE

1/4" X 5 1/2" SQ. TOP AND BOTTOM

1/8" X 3/4" PEGS (8) LOCK TOP AND BOTTOM

strip is placed under the long slot cut into the top. Make sure the strips are located so there is clearance for the vertical posts.

Now slip three of the side shields into their grooves. The fourth side can slide in later from the top through the slot.

The lamp socket, of the type shown, is attached to the top by screwing on the porcelain cap onto the socket threads, after the lamp cord is connected to the socket terminals. A piece of metal, cut from a tin coffee can, is bent into a curve and nailed to the top, serving as a vent hood. Small holes drilled in this metal hold the bail handle, made of thin rod.

With a pocket knife chamfer the front corners of the posts and round off the edges of the plates for a rustic effect. Hang the lantern on a wall with a simple metal bracket. •

Two-Tier End Table

A decorative piece used for reading light, storage and convenient table

ALWAYS a favorite with Early American enthusiasts, the two-tier chairside table is a particularly functional piece of furniture.

The entire unit is made of plain, easy-to-work pine boards. The only intricate jointing is with the legs which are doweled to the shelf skirting.

The table is made in two sections: the base including the large shelf, and the top drawer section which fits at the back over projecting dowels.

The legs are made first, of standard 2-by 2-inch pine stock, 15 inches long. They are tapered on only the two inner sides, down to a slim 1- by 1-inch square. This is easy to do on a circular saw with a taper jig made of two hinged boards, as shown in a drawing. The legs will be set in, about ½ inch from each corner edge.

Make the bottom shelf according to the diagram to 17- by 26½-inch size by edge-gluing two pieces of 1- by 9-inch stock, and chamfering or sanding the end-grain edge at the front. Compute from this the lengths of the 3-inch-wide skirting which will join the four legs. Make the curved cuts along an edge, then join the legs and four skirting rails by "blind doweling" and gluing.

The large shelf is attached to the base with ¼-inch dowels in holes drilled through the top into the side skirting rails. Near the front, the dowels are cut off flush, but the dowels near the back are allowed to extend about ¾ inch above the shelf. These will act as anchors for the upper section. The latter will be drilled to match the projecting dowel ends.

The drawer section is made of five parts: the two sides, the back which fits between the sides, a lower shelf which is set into dadoes grooved into the sides, and the top shelf that slightly overhangs the sides. The two shelves form an opening for one or two drawers, according to taste. Drawings show measurements for two drawers.

The top shelf of this section is secured with glued dowels which protrude about ¾ inch above the shelf to secure the shaped 3-side topmost edging.

The drawer has a fully recessed front, made of the same ¾-inch stock, but the drawer sides, back and bottom should be of thinner material if available. Use round wood knobs. •

The two-step table done in soft pine is a worthy chairside companion with accommodations for needed articles.

The legs are tapered on two sides only to a slim one inch square at the bottom. Use a tapering jig on a table saw.

Top section has an interesting profile design. Draw the curved side on heavy paper and trace directly on wood.

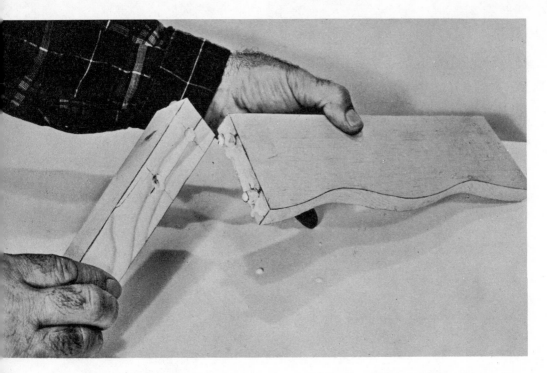

Legs are joined to shelf skirting by blind doweling glued together. Drill dowel holes at center lines.

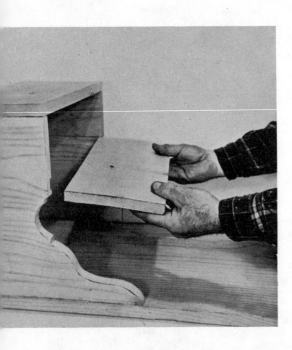

The center shelf is held in dado grooves that are cut into the sides to form the drawer compartment.

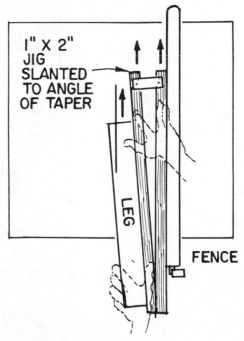

RIPPING A LEG TAPER

1" X 2" JIG SLANTED TO ANGLE OF TAPER

LEG

FENCE

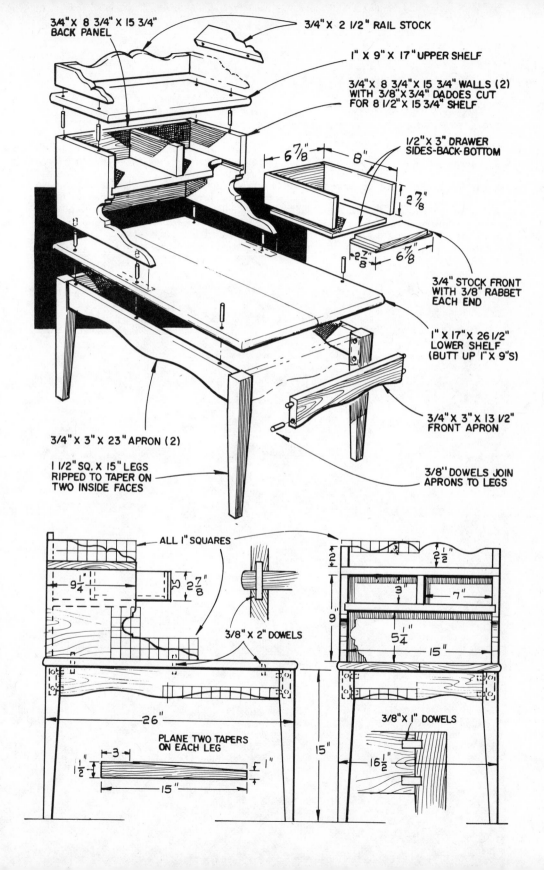

3/4" X 8 3/4" X 15 3/4"
BACK PANEL

3/4" X 2 1/2" RAIL STOCK

1" X 9" X 17" UPPER SHELF

3/4" X 8 3/4" X 15 3/4" WALLS (2)
WITH 3/8" X 3/4" DADOES CUT
FOR 8 1/2" X 15 3/4" SHELF

1/2" X 3" DRAWER
SIDES-BACK-BOTTOM

6 7/8"   8"

2 7/8"

2 7/8"   6 7/8"

3/4" STOCK FRONT
WITH 3/8" RABBET
EACH END

1" X 17" X 26 1/2"
LOWER SHELF
(BUTT UP 1" X 9"S)

3/4" X 3" X 13 1/2"
FRONT APRON

3/4" X 3" X 23" APRON (2)

1 1/2" SQ. X 15" LEGS
RIPPED TO TAPER ON
TWO INSIDE FACES

3/8" DOWELS JOIN
APRONS TO LEGS

ALL 1" SQUARES

9 1/4"   2 7/8"

3/8" X 2" DOWELS

2 1/2"

2 1/2"

3

7"

9"

5 1/4"

15"

26"

PLANE TWO TAPERS
ON EACH LEG

1 1/2"   3   1"

15"

15"

3/8" X 1" DOWELS

16 1/2"

Hutch Cabinet

This adaptation is useful as a serving buffet and refreshment bar

HUTCH CABINETS are of particular interest to Early American "buffs" who appreciate the infinite variety of design within the confines of that simple basic form.

A dry sink, with its deep enclosed shelf, has been adapted here as a serving buffet and refreshment bar. An apothecary shelf holds interesting spice jars, and the three drawers above are quite useful for small items. The lower compartments store large trays and silver service.

Ordinary 1-inch ponderosa pine stock, selected for pleasing grain pattern and a few sound knots, is used for all but the large shelves—which are of ¾-inch plywood, and the back—which is of ¼-inch plywood. The pine, stained and rubbed to

a rich patina, has a remarkable quality in that its appearance is enhanced by the knots, minor dents and even scratches which in other woods would be considered objectionable blemishes.

The two sides are the key members, dadoed to support the shelves that hold the unit together. As the width of these sides exceeds that of standard board lumber, the first step is to edge-glue two boards to get the required 17 inches overall width for each side.

Study the drawings to observe the dimensions and configurations of these sides. Overall height is 59 inches. Since only the lower half of the side is the full width, cut an 8-inch-wide board to 32½-inch length. Shape out the front projection which is an angle 1 inch deep and 4½ inches long. When this is completed, edge-glue it to a full-length 1- by 10-inch board, then rip down the longer side to get the 17-inch total width.

Rabbet the back edges for recessing the ¼-inch rear panel and cut the required dadoes ¼ inch deep for the shelf inserts as spaced in the drawings, including an extra shelf inside the cupboards if desired. Remember that the shelves in the lower section will be of ¾ inch thickness, while

At left, cabinet is a focal point for any Early American room. Beautiful finish improves with age.

At right, the cabinet sides are made by blind doweling and edge-gluing different sized boards.

Below, left: Use clamps to draw edges together, but do not tighten too much or joint may buckle.

Bottom right: Pattern is taken from diagram on paper and traced directly on sides for cutting.

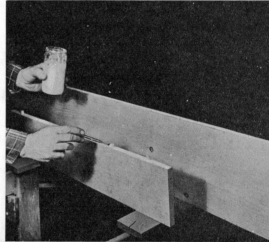

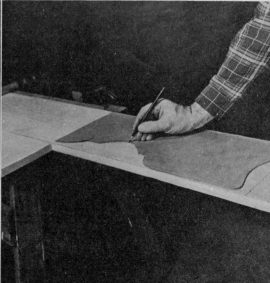

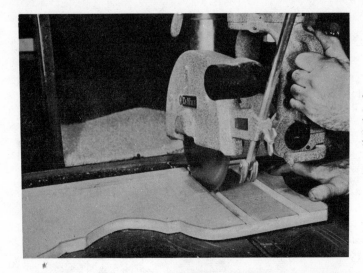

The inner side sections are dadoed for the two large and three small shelves, and the rear inner edges are rabbeted for the 1/4-inch plywood panel.

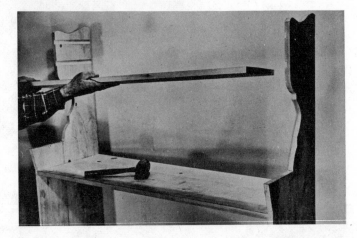

Start assembly with the two larger bottom shelves. Top shelves may either be pre assembled with the drawer dividers, or finished later.

the exposed upper shelves will be of somewhat thicker solid pine stock, so make the grooves accordingly. Then make the profile cuts into the sides with a jig saw or coping saw, smoothly rounding the edges.

Cut two plywood shelves, 15¾ by 51 inches, and drive them into the dadoes at the bottom and the sink top levels between the sides, leaving clearance for the back panel. Cut and attach the back panel 53 inches long, and wide enough to fit between the sides, or 51½ inches. Fasten it so the bottom is flush with the lower shelf.

The sink shelf is enclosed at the front with a board 4½ inches wide, beveled on the bottom edge, and attached with finishing nails. The spice shelf and top fascia board are cut and fitted into place, but the drawer section may first be assembled with the drawer dividers before installation.

The lower compartments are finished off, as shown in the drawings, with three vertical facing boards nailed in place, followed by the scroll-cut base trim of the same stock.

The two doors are embellished with bevel-edge panels, each 13½ by 17½ inches, inserted into surrounding 3-inch frames. The bevels are cut all around on the circular saw with the blade tilted, and the panels are inserted into rabbets cut into the frames. Attach the doors with black iron LH hinges, and fit simple wood knobs and latches.

When completed, the hutch is finished with oil stain applied at one time to the entire surface, unless you prefer to paint the back panel for contrast. Removable serving trays or metal planter boxes may be built to fit the dry sink shelf. •

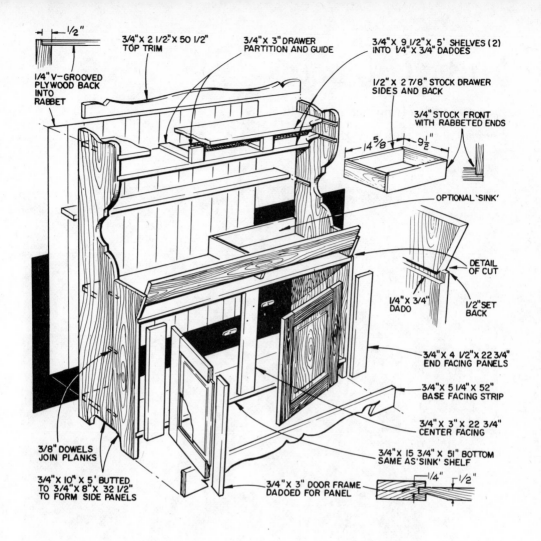

1/2"

1/4" V-GROOVED PLYWOOD BACK INTO RABBET

3/4" x 2 1/2" x 50 1/2" TOP TRIM

3/4" x 3" DRAWER PARTITION AND GUIDE

3/4" x 9 1/2" x 5' SHELVES (2) INTO 1/4" x 3/4" DADOES

1/2" x 2 7/8" STOCK DRAWER SIDES AND BACK

3/4" STOCK FRONT WITH RABBETED ENDS

14 5/8"   9 1/2"

OPTIONAL 'SINK'

DETAIL OF CUT

1/4" x 3/4" DADO

1/2" SET BACK

3/4" x 4 1/2" x 22 3/4" END FACING PANELS

3/4" x 5 1/4" x 52" BASE FACING STRIP

3/4" x 3" x 22 3/4" CENTER FACING

3/4" x 15 3/4" x 51" BOTTOM SAME AS 'SINK' SHELF

3/8" DOWELS JOIN PLANKS

3/4" x 10" x 5' BUTTED TO 3/4" x 8" x 32 1/2" TO FORM SIDE PANELS

3/4" x 3" DOOR FRAME DADOED FOR PANEL

1/4"   1/2"

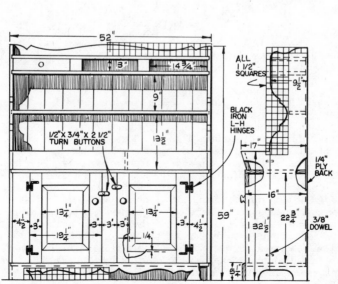

52"

3"   4 3/4"

9"

1/2" x 3/4" x 2 1/2" TURN BUTTONS

13 1/2"

ALL 1 1/2" SQUARES

9 1/2"

BLACK IRON L-H HINGES

17"

1/4" PLY BACK

13 1/4"

13 1/4"

4 1/2" 3"   3" 3"   3" 4 1/2"

19 1/4"

1/4"

59"

16"

32 1/2"

22 3/4"

3/8" DOWEL

5 1/4"

45

Music Cabinet

The styling and finishing complement a room paneled in knotty pine

Spacious pine cabinet holds many record albums,
and curved face board makes them easy to reach.

THIS free-swinging music cabinet is particularly suitable for the informal den or family room, of which so many are finished in knotty pine wall paneling. The colorful record albums are exposed like books—and just as handy to reach. The two small drawers will be useful for keeping phonograph accessories.

Regular 1- by 12-inch pine shelving, or No. 2 common grade in ponderosa pine or Idaho white pine, are used. You'll need a total of 16 square feet, plus a 2- by 2-foot plywood section for the back panel and some ½-inch and ¼-inch stock for the drawers. Construction involves some dado

grooving and will seem very complicated, but, taken step by step, it is not a difficult project.

First make the front facing board, with its two arches and the drawer openings, from a board 9 by 24½ inches, copying the curve of the arches from the drawings, and cutting the drawer openings with a jig saw or keyhole saw. This facing board is grooved at the back to receive the center divider panel of the cabinet. Round off the edges of this board.

Next, saw the three vertical panels from full 1 by 12 stock. The two outside panels, each 25 inches long, are ripped part way

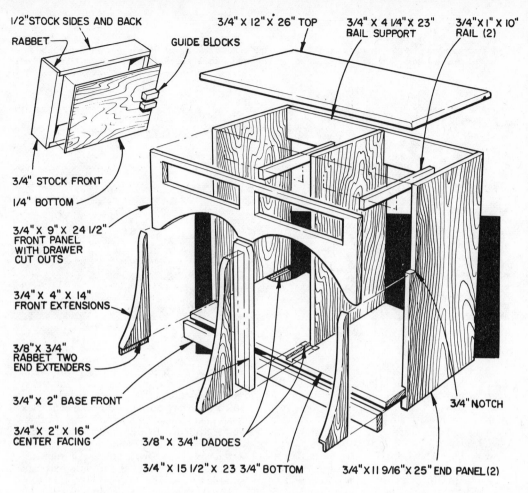

1/2" STOCK SIDES AND BACK

RABBET

GUIDE BLOCKS

3/4" X 12" X 26" TOP

3/4" X 4 1/4" X 23" BAIL SUPPORT

3/4" X 1" X 10" RAIL (2)

3/4" STOCK FRONT

1/4" BOTTOM

3/4" X 9" X 24 1/2" FRONT PANEL WITH DRAWER CUT OUTS

3/4" X 4" X 14" FRONT EXTENSIONS

3/8" X 3/4" RABBET TWO END EXTENDERS

3/4" X 2" BASE FRONT

3/4" X 2" X 16" CENTER FACING

3/8" X 3/4" DADOES

3/4" X 15 1/2" X 23 3/4" BOTTOM

3/4" NOTCH

3/4" X 11 9/16" X 25" END PANEL (2)

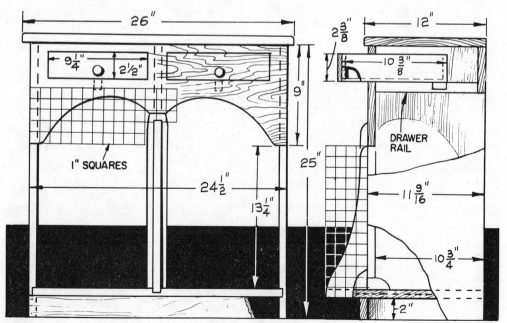

26"

9 1/4"

2 1/2"

1" SQUARES

24 1/2"

9"

25"

13 1/4"

2 3/8"

12"

10 3/8"

DRAWER RAIL

11 9/16"

10 3/4"

2"

47

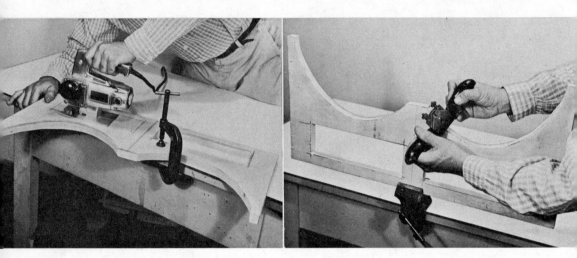

A pattern is used to mark all cutting lines on the face board. A saber saw, left, or a keyhole saw makes cutouts, started by drilling holes in corners, and a spokeshave, right, rounds off all the edges.

down at the top end to form a notch ¾ inch deep, 9 inches long, to recess the arched facing board. The middle upright is only 23¼ inches long, as it will rest in a groove of the bottom shelf, and is narrower, ripped down to receive a ½-inch strip. The end panels receive 25/32-inch dado cuts two inches above the bottom edge for this shelf. Another detail: the middle upright is notched one inch deep at the top end to support a 1- by 4-inch board that will fit across the back to hold the drawer rails. This 1 by 4, in turn, is mortised at two places for the one-inch drawer rails, centered at each half section.

The bottom shelf is wider than your 12-inch stock, so a 3½-inch strip must be added. Cut the shelf to 15½-inch length, the same with the extra 3½-inch strip, and butt joint the parts together by edge-gluing. This glued joint will be reinforced by the base front stretcher that will go directly underneath. In this bottom shelf, make a shallow dado groove down the center wide enough to take the middle upright. Now you can assemble most of the cabinet. Slip the bottom shelf into the grooves of the side uprights, set in the top stretcher across the back and nail it to the sides.

Add the 2-inch-wide base front stretcher across the bottom, nailing it to the end uprights and also down through the bottom shelf. Set the middle upright into its shelf groove flush with the back edge of the shelf. Cut the top, 26 inches long, and nail it securely to the side and middle uprights,

the back stretcher, and the front facing.

Now come the ornamental front extensions, which are shaped according to the ruled diagram, but note that the center extension is somewhat higher than the others, and is attached to a narrow plate that goes over the edge of the middle divider. These extensions are rabbeted at the bottom to go against the shelf, but the middle extension slips into the center groove of this shelf.

The back panel, either of solid stock like the rest, or of ¾-inch plywood, is cut to fit the space below the drawer rail stretcher, and simply tacked on. The drawer rails, 1"x1", are 10 inches long, fitted into the rear notch, and held with a single finishing nail through the front. They must be lined up true, front to back.

Make the drawer, as shown in drawings, to fit the openings, using the same wood stock as the cabinet. The drawers, 2⅜ inches deep, are given short guide blocks underneath at the back which will hold the drawers to their rails. These guide blocks should be short enough so that they will clear the opening when the drawer is tilted all the way down, permitting the drawer to enter. The guide blocks also keep the drawer from accidentally falling out.

Final touches now consist of countersetting all nailheads, rounding and chamfering all exposed end grain and corners to reduce the bulky appearance and to give the cabinet a rustic country appearance. Sand thoroughly and finish with penetrating oil stain in a light maple color. •

Candle Box Planter

A decorative piece for the family room, the dining area or kitchen

IN THE OLDEN DAYS a wall box like this one would be used as the receptacle for the household supply of precious wax tapers. With a kindly thought to our forebears, we adapt this quaint design to present-day purpose as a container for fresh-cut flowers, or a planter. The bottom drawer, with waterproof liner, is suitable for raising philodendron plants (vines).

You'll find it doubly interesting to make this little item yourself, fashioning the

Candle boxes are no longer required, but this item of long-past days makes a good-looking wall planter, holds glass jar for fresh-cut flowers.

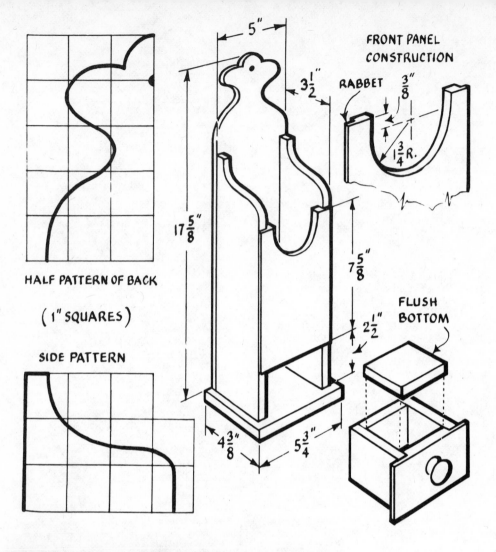

HALF PATTERN OF BACK

(1" SQUARES)

SIDE PATTERN

5"

3½"

FRONT PANEL
CONSTRUCTION

RABBET

⅜"

1¾ R.

17⅝"

7⅝"

2½"

FLUSH
BOTTOM

4⅜"

5¾"

Front panel is sawn for
rabbet to fit over the side
edges. Two or three passes
made over a shallow-set
saw blade does the job.

parts with a small coping saw. The wood should be ½-inch-thick soft pine which is sold at most lumberyards.

Though very soft and easy to saw, the wood sands to perfect smoothness and is beautifully finished with penetrating stain and wax. The project will be done much more easily, and with better final results, if the wood stock is sanded smooth while in a large piece.

The box parts are nailed together with small brads. No complicated clamping is necessary. The wood may have small, tight knots, or even deep gouges. These accentuate the pine wood, and strangely, even improve the appearance of this rugged wood.

Start by cutting the wood for the back panel, 5 by 17⅝ inches long, and the two sides, each 3½ inches wide and 12¾ inches long. Each piece must be sawed or planed square along the sides. Make cardboard patterns of the scrolled contours by tracing from the design shown in 1-inch squares. Trace the pattern outlines directly on the wood pieces. Since the two sides are identical, they may be cut out simultaneously by nailing them together.

Join the back and two sides with nails through the back, making sure that the bottom edges of all three parts are perfectly flush. Saw an insert shelf, about 3⅜ by 4¼ inches, to fit inside the opening, and nail it in place 2½ inches above the bottom. The back and sides are now held more securely and the bottom may now be

nailed on. This is 4⅜ by 5¾ inches, thus overlapping the box on three sides. One edge is flush with the back.

The front panel will fit and look better if the edges are rabbeted so the panel will be recessed into the opening and just a narrow strip remains showing along the front edge. This rabbeting requires a circular saw, or at least a combination plane with special cutters. But you can avoid all that by just fitting a thin ¼-inch panel over the front, cut to the rounded shape at the top as shown, and fitted over the insert shelf at the bottom.

This leaves a 2½-inch opening at the bottom for a small drawer which will be ideal for the philodendron. The drawer may be lined with aluminum foil or vinyl plastic sheeting to hold soil and retain water.

The drawer may be of basic design when made with hand tools; the front is merely cut to fit into the drawer opening and the other drawer parts cut and joined to fit. When made with power tools, however, the drawer front should be rabbeted to leave just a small overlap at the sides. The drawer parts are firmly nailed together. Use a typical old-fashioned wood knob for the drawer.

The top section is large enough to place a tall glass or jar inside on the hidden shelf for keeping fresh flowers in water. When the bottom drawer is used as a planter box with a foil liner, be careful about the amount of water used. •

Front of drawer may be cut back for overlap on sides, or simply made to fit flush into opening.

Use penetrating stain and wax for a finish. The drawer is lined to hold soil and to retain water.

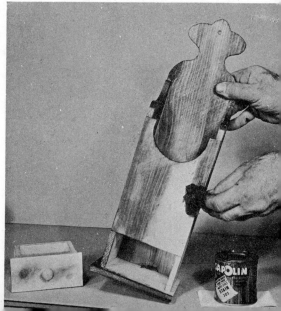

Sewing Screen

The sewing screen opens to stand conveniently at hand while you work, is easily carried, and folds flat to two-inch thickness for storage in closets.

A portable cabinet which holds all sewing material required in the home

THIS SEWING cabinet, so light you can carry it in one hand, holds as many spools of thread as you may ever need (center will take about 64 spools) plus scissors, tape, buttons and needles. A small-print fabric covers the outside of the screen, and there are elastic pockets of contrasting material to hold odds and ends of sewing equipment such as ribbons, zippers, etc. The top of each side will have a sturdy rope handle so the screen can be easily carried.

The screen requires about 21 feet of 1½- by 1½-inch clear lumber plus a small piece of ¼-inch stock for the shelf and about 7 or 8 feet of ¼-inch dowel. Start by sawing the lumber to size. Cut four pieces 30½ inches long, seven pieces 12½

inches long, and two pieces 14½ inches long.

Place the four longest pieces on a table side by side. Starting at one end rule lines, across all pieces, six inches apart. Pencil a check mark on all four pieces at the end where they are flush so you won't mix them up later. Hold a ruler at the ½-inch position, across each of the lines, and mark a cross line which will give the center point at each position.

Drill pilot holes for 1½-inch No. 8 screws at each of the cross marks, except the next to the bottom one, on one side, since that is where the elastic pocket will go. Countersink the holes so the screw heads won't show.

Before assembling drill four of the cross

Four crosspieces are cut 12¼ inches long and drilled along the center line for dowels used for spools.

The sides are predrilled and countersunk to recess the screw heads. Holes are covered with wood filler.

When the two sections are completed they are joined with butt hinges, allowing clearance for hinge pins.

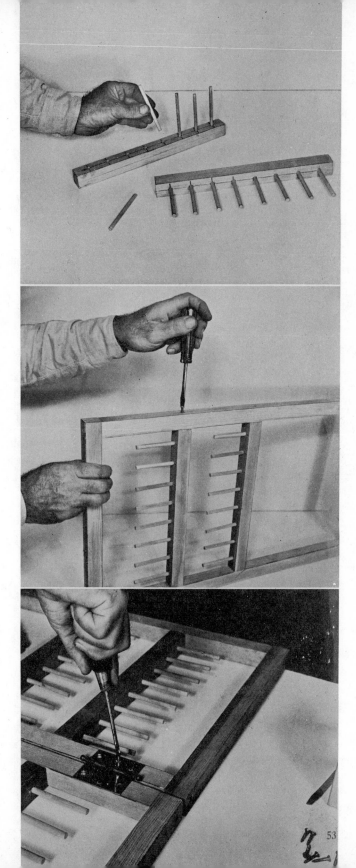

53

Shelf has finger-grip cut-out at top, is held with small hinges. Chains hold it in the desired position.

Lower sections are fitted with cloth pockets having elastic bands at the top to hold ribbons and tapes.

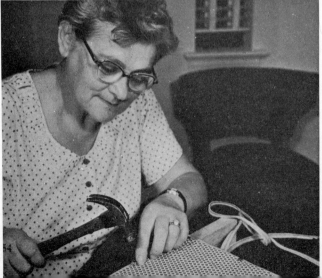

The sewing screens are enclosed at the back with attractive panels tacked on with upholstery nails.

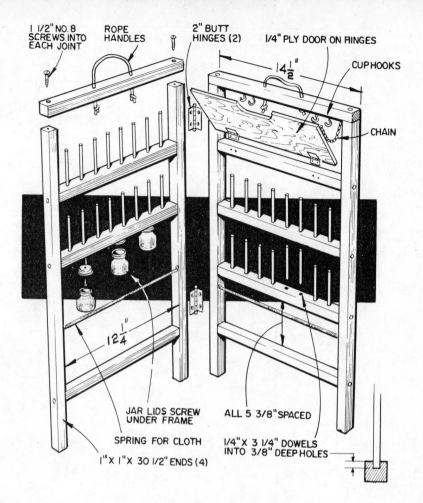

1 1/2" NO. 8 SCREWS INTO EACH JOINT

ROPE HANDLES

2" BUTT HINGES (2)

1/4" PLY DOOR ON HINGES

14 1/2"

CUP HOOKS

CHAIN

12 1/4"

JAR LIDS SCREW UNDER FRAME

ALL 5 3/8" SPACED

SPRING FOR CLOTH

1" X 1" X 30 1/2" ENDS (4)

1/4" X 3 1/4" DOWELS INTO 3/8" DEEP HOLES

members for ¼-inch dowel pegs, placing the holes as shown in the drawing. Each cross member has eight holes, ½ inch deep. Dip the dowel ends in glue before driving them into the holes. Rounding the ends of the pegs with sandpaper will make it easier to put on the spools.

Now join the sides of the cross members, placing them as shown to leave room for the two pockets and drop-leaf shelf. To locate the parts square and level, saw two pieces of scrap stock to 5⅜-inch length, using them as spacers so the position is equal on both sides. Drive in the screws tightly.

Drill end holes in the 14½-inch lengths, and attach them at the top with screws to complete the basic frame. The shelf is added next, 5 inches wide, and 12¼ inches long, to fit the top section. Saw a recess in a long edge for finger grip and attach the shelf with hinges to the crosspiece.

Join the halves of the screen with two 2-inch butt hinges. This is done best by placing the sections together on a table.

Put the hinges on the inside with the leaves opened across the uprights. Separate the frames about a quarter inch to allow for the hinge pin, then turn in the screws to hold the hinges. A neater way is to cut shallow gains with a chisel in the uprights to recess the hinge leaves, but this is not necessary. The screen should open and fold easily; if not, the hinges are not straight and should be reset.

Finally, drill two holes at the top on each side for the rope handles. The pockets are made with elastic bands at the top and fastened to the sides and bottom with tacks or a stapler. Or, make a fold at the top of the pockets and run a spring through it. Attach the spring at the sides with screws. Do this before tacking on the outside fabric covering which is backed with corrugated cardboard. Place decorative welt strips along the outside edges to cover the tacks. The button bottles are attached to the underside of a cross-member by drilling holes in the metal caps and fastening them with screws. •

Wood is easy to sand to perfect smoothness, has attractive graining which is emphasized by the stain.

Three-Drawer Wall Case

A decorative addition to any home, made from thin quarter-inch scrap pine wood

THIS AUTHENTIC wall case imparts the real Early American flavor, makes a decorative addition to any home. And it can be done with ¼-inch-thick pine which can be found in discarded fruit boxes.

Avoid splitting the wood when you break up the box. Pull out the nails after tapping the board sufficiently to bring out the nailheads just far enough for a claw hammer to grasp them. The box lumber is ¼ inch thick, except for the ends, which will be either ½ or ¾ inch thick. These will be fine for the drawer fronts.

You will need four pieces of ¼-inch stock about 5x18 inches in size, which, when cut to size and shape, will make up the three shelves and the back fascia board. You will also need two pieces 5x16 inches for the vertical members, which will have to be cut to shape. For the rest, just small pieces of wood from the box will suffice. The wood, if from a fruit box, may be quite rough, but you'll be agreeably surprised to see how smoothly it can be sanded. If you can't find a wood box (they're scarce these days) use regular ¼- or ⅜-inch stock.

Start by laying out the profile patterns

of the sides and the top fascia board on a grid of 1-inch squares (see drawing). Trace the outline on the wood. Both sides are identical, so you can nail the sides together temporarily and cut them simultaneously with a jig or band saw, or with a hand coping saw.

The inner sides are grooved at three places as indicated in the drawing, to receive the shelves. These grooves, done with dado blades, are very shallow and just wide enough to receive the shelf stock. Make these dado grooves before cutting the pattern profile in the sides so there'll be no error of position.

The top shelf is plain, sawed to 3¾ by 17⅞ inches, while the two lower shelves are 5 by 17⅞ inches. The bottom of the middle shelf and the top of the bottom shelf are grooved across at two places to divide the shelf into three equal parts. The grooves should match, top and bottom, to receive ½- by 3- by 5-inch vertical partitions which act as drawer guides. For

Transfer profile designs from paper pattern for top fascia, scalloped front trim and two sides.

Place stock on a bench or board and make it immovable, held down with a C-clamp while cutting.

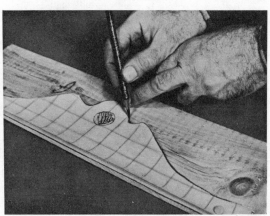

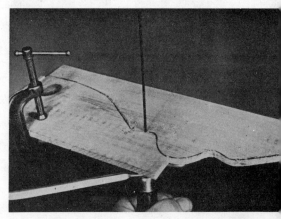

Sides are dadoed to hold the shelves. The lower shelves are also grooved to hold drawer dividers.

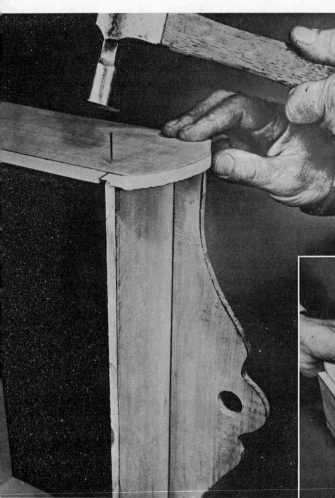

Join shelves to sides by nailing with wire brads and counterset the heads. Drawer guide dividers are set in grooves and nailed in.

The drawer fronts are rabbeted on the edges, the sides nailed in and the back cut to fit. The bottom is glued and then nailed.

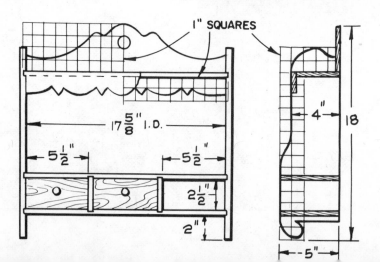

1" SQUARES

$17\frac{5}{8}$" I.D.

$5\frac{1}{2}$"

$5\frac{1}{2}$"

$2\frac{1}{2}$"

2"

4"

18

5"

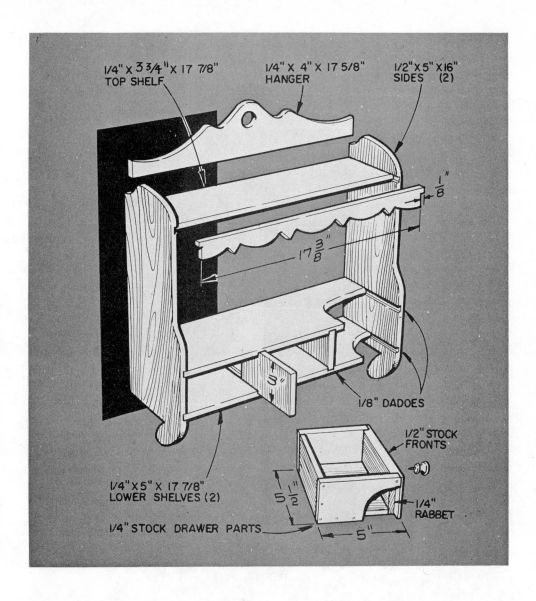

1/4" x 3 3/4" x 17 7/8"
TOP SHELF

1/4" x 4" x 17 5/8"
HANGER

1/2" x 5" x 16"
SIDES (2)

1/8"

17 3/8"

3"

1/8" DADOES

1/2" STOCK
FRONTS

1/4" x 5" x 17 7/8"
LOWER SHELVES (2)

5 1/2"

1/4"
RABBET

1/4" STOCK DRAWER PARTS

5"

uniformity, make the shelf grooves before ripping the wood to shelf width. Nail the shelves into the grooves with 1-inch wire brads.

The back fascia board is sawed to shape from one piece of the 5-inch-wide stock, drilled for a 1-inch hole at the center position, and nailed in between the sides with finishing nails.

Now for the drawers, of which there are three all alike. They are made to fit loosely into the openings. Cut three drawer fronts of ½-inch stock to size of the drawer opening, approximately 2½ by 5½ inches. Cut a rabbet ¼ inch deep along each edge

of the drawer fronts for receiving the sides.

A piece is fitted between the sides at the back, and the drawer bottom of ¼-inch stock goes neatly into the opening, nailed in on three sides with brads. The three drawers are just the right size for keeping decks of cards and other game materials. Put on small brass knobs for drawer pulls and add on the scalloped molding at the front, over the top shelf edge, dadoed to fit the side grooves.

For finishing, select any light wood stain of the penetrating oil type, brush it on and allow to stand for a few minutes, then wipe off with a cloth. •

Knitting Box

A present-day application of an old-time functional piece of furniture

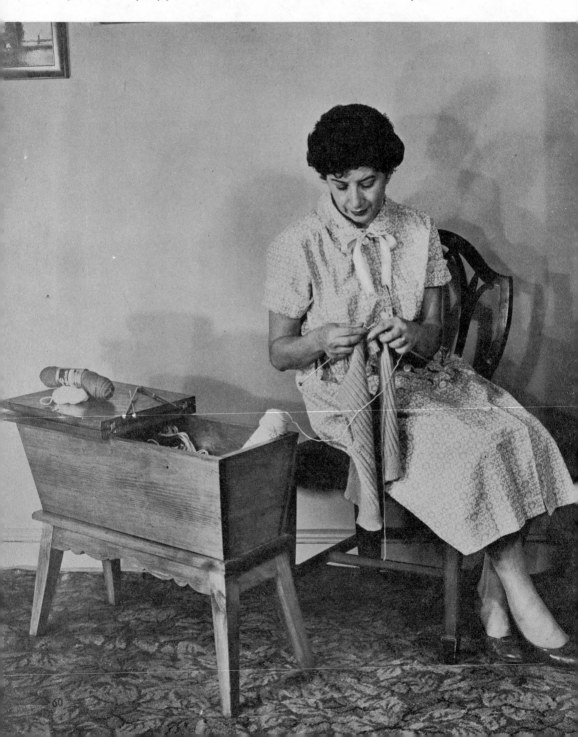

E VEN IN THESE DAYS of store-bought, precooked and packaged victuals there are many old-timers who recall nostalgically the aromatic bread-baking sessions when the dough box stood in a kitchen corner and all walked softly lest the dough "fall." While little bread baking is done nowadays, alas, the dough box retains a fond place in our homes.

This memento of times past has practical present-day applications because of its spacious interior, with convenient surface lids. A favored use is that of knitting or sewing box, where work in process can be kept undisturbed together with all the necessary supplies. Making a similar dough box is an interesting and worthwhile project.

Use common pine board, selected for grain and knots to individual preference. About 10 feet of 1x10-inch board should be sufficient, plus about five feet of heavier stock from which you can obtain the 2x2-inch legs. Edge-glued boards will give the 12x26-inch size needed for the two-part lid.

The legs are tapered on two sides, on a power saw or with a hand plane, and splayed to slope slightly in two directions. This sounds like a complicated process, but actually it is accomplished by a simple technique which enables you to turn out the required parts quickly and easily.

The legs are ripped to uniform 2x2-inch thickness and cut to 12¾-inch length. On the bench saw, set the miter gauge to 82 degrees, which is just a slight variation from the normal 90-degree setting.

Draw a single diagonal line across the end of the leg, from corner to corner. Place the leg against the miter fence and align the diagonal with a try square so it is vertical and plumb. Hold the leg tightly against the back fence with the nearest corner of the wood touching the inside tooth of the saw blade. Run the work through the blade. Repeat this for the rest of the legs, and all will have a "high spot" at one corner. This angle-cutting also may be done with a

Left, the dough box, treasured for its neat lines and warm appearance, serves as a container for knitting materials.

A simple taper jig used to slim down legs on two sides. Jig rips all legs uniformly, does the work very quickly.

End pieces are cut at 82° so top is larger than the bottom. When parts are joined, top edges are planed down flush.

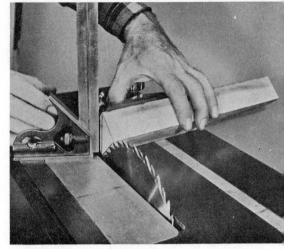

Rails are outlined from pattern made by tracing lines on 1" squares. Cut with a jig or band saw.

To angle-cut the legs for two-way slant, plumb a diagonal line with a try square and cut at 82°.

The bottom platform completed, the sides of top section are attached with screws from underneath.

back saw in a miter box, or free hand on marked guide lines.

For tapering the legs, run them through the saw with a taper jig set at a slight angle. The setting is not critical, but the jig should be locked so all legs are cut uniformly. Make two taper cuts on adjacent sides of each leg, so that the bottom end, opposite the angle-cut end, will finally be narrowed to about 1½x1½ inches. When taper is cut with a plane, mark the guide lines on all four sides of each leg to assure a perfect joint.

The platform is a plain piece of stock, 9¼x25⅜ inches. The legs are attached to the corners with screws through the platform into the leg ends which will hold together until the scroll-shaped rails are made and joined into the assembly. The sketch shows the decorative profile of these rails, but they must be fitted into place and attached with screws through the platform. These screw heads are covered when the top section is put on.

The ends of all four sides of the dough box are cut with the 82-degree saw setting, or chamfered with a plane, to give the flared appearance of the top. When the parts are joined, the top edges will not be level and should be planed down for neat appearance. Simple nailing will do for this assembly, and attaching to the platform is done with several long but thin screws (1½ inch No. 8) from underneath, where they will not show.

The lid is in two equal parts, joined at the center with hinges. Only one lid will lift; the other is permanently secured. Butt hinges may be used with the hinge pins showing along the joining line, but this can be avoided by using one of the hidden-type hinges, such as the Soss hinge, which has a telescoping action and is recessed into the edge mortises.

For a mellow appearance, trim the square edges, particularly those of the platform, with a cornering tool. A few shallow dents made with a peen hammer will give an antique effect. Finish the wood with oil stain. •

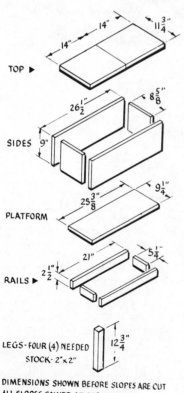

TOP ▶

14" 14" 11¾"

SIDES 26½" 8⅝" 9"

PLATFORM 25⅜" 9¼"

RAILS ▶ 21" 5¼" 2½"

LEGS-FOUR (4) NEEDED
STOCK- 2"x2" 12¾"

DIMENSIONS SHOWN BEFORE SLOPES ARE CUT
ALL SLOPES SAWED AT 82° SETTING

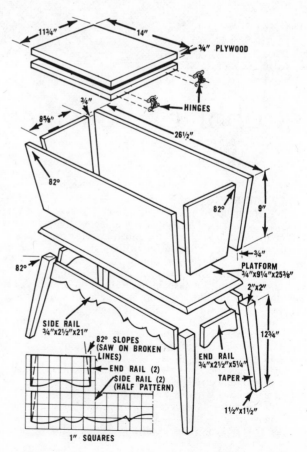

11¾" 14" ¾" PLYWOOD

¾" HINGES

8½" 26½"

82° 82° 9"

82° ¾" PLATFORM
¾"x9¼"x25⅜"
2"x2"

SIDE RAIL
¾"x2½"x21"

82° SLOPES
(SAW ON BROKEN LINES)

END RAIL (2)
SIDE RAIL (2)
(HALF PATTERN)

END RAIL
¾"x2½"x5¼"

TAPER ▶

1½"x1½"

12¾"

1" SQUARES

63

Cobbler's Bench

A workbench of the past is adapted for use in the modern living room

THE RUGGED old cobbler's bench has come up in the world! Now it serves as a cocktail table to grace handsome living rooms. It is one of the more interesting examples of a strictly utilitarian item adapted for decorative purposes. Because of its sound proportions, its interesting contours and the association with long-ago days, the cobbler's bench is very popular among collectors of Early American replicas.

Whether of soft pine, dented and made to look blackened with age, or in smooth and gleaming maple, the cobbler's bench is still a conversation piece, particularly when made of very old wood, salvaged perhaps from an old barn or floor planks.

This coffee table combines sturdy basic construction with "light" frills on top such as the sliding cover planter section, the

"dished" ring at one end, and the useful little compartments. An ample drawer underneath will be found handy for entertainment accessories such as playing cards, chessmen, etc., or coasters and cigarettes.

When made of pine, the soft wood is easily fashioned to the various shapes. Joining is done with screws hidden with plug inserts cut from dowels. Maple is more difficult to work, requiring real sharp tools for careful jointing and gluing.

The first problem is to get a board of the right thickness and at least 15 inches wide for the bench top. The board should be a full one inch thick (referred to as 5/4 stock) rather than the usual ¾-inch board. This may be obtained in 8- or 10-inch width, so it will be necessary to glue up two pieces edge to edge. When gluing, place the boards together on a table with waxed

The informal cobbler's bench rivals the coffee table designs of other periods for popularity as furniture for living room.

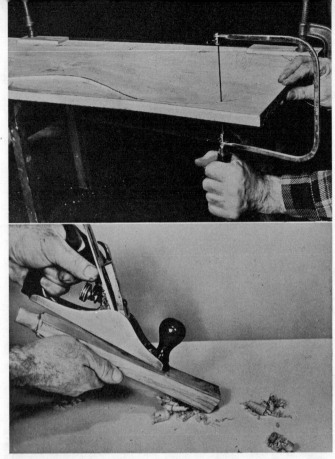

Top is cut in traditional shape with a coping saw. The glued boards are re-enforced by two cleats attached from underneath.

After marking guide lines the four legs are "reverse tapered" on the outside only, to give them an appearance of outward slope.

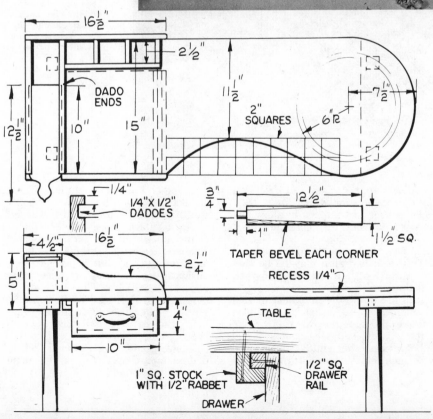

16½"

2½"

DADO ENDS

11½"

7½"

12½"

10"

15"

2" SQUARES

6"R

1/4"

1/4" X 1/2" DADOES

3/4"

12½"

1"

1½" SQ.

TAPER BEVEL EACH CORNER

RECESS 1/4"

4½"

16½"

2¼"

5"

4"

10"

TABLE

1" SQ. STOCK WITH 1/2" RABBET

1/2" SQ. DRAWER RAIL

DRAWER

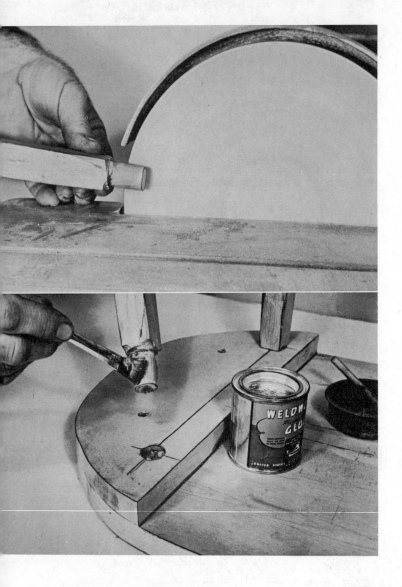

The leg ends are tenoned for a ¾-inch hole. Tenons can be whittled roughly and then rounded by turning against a disc sander.

Legs are glued into holes drilled two inches from the sides into the cleat. Make sure that auger does not pierce upper surface.

paper underneath, put clamps at each end to hold the center line down flush, then apply clamp pressure uniformly along the outside edges to bring the center together.

The top board, 40 inches long, is then shaped out as shown in the drawings. At this time, the dished ring may be gouged out, if desired, with a chisel to ¼-inch depth at the lowest part.

The ends are of double thickness to give better support for the leg tenons, and also to reinforce the glued up boards of the bench top. At one end, the cleat is 1- by 4-inch board; the other end is shaped from 1- by 8-inch stock to conform to the

rounded end of the bench top. These cleats are fitted flush with the top along the outside edges, in keeping with the design.

The legs are of 1½- by 1½-inch stock, of the same kind of wood as the bench top. The legs are set in straight, that is, at right angle to the top, but appear to be sloped outward because they are tapered upward on the outside only. Thus they are slightly narrower at the top. The tapering is done with a plane after guide lines are marked along the leg edges. All corners of the legs are rounded.

The leg ends are tenoned to fit holes drilled into cleats. You might turn these

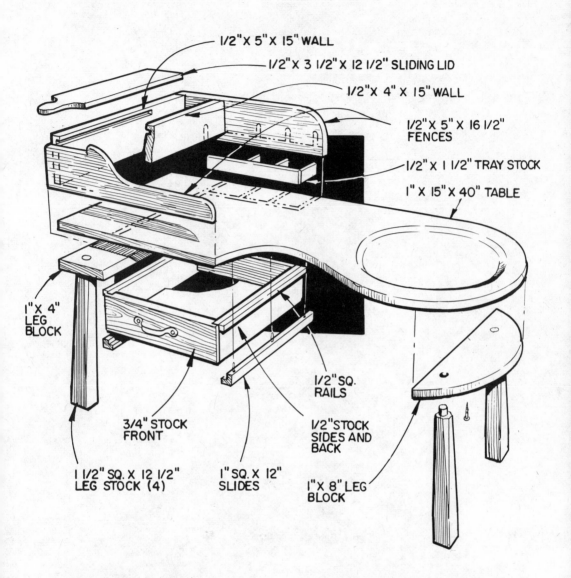

1/2" X 5" X 15" WALL

1/2" X 3 1/2" X 12 1/2" SLIDING LID

1/2" X 4" X 15" WALL

1/2" X 5" X 16 1/2" FENCES

1/2" X 1 1/2" TRAY STOCK

1" X 15" X 40" TABLE

1" X 4" LEG BLOCK

1/2" SQ. RAILS

3/4" STOCK FRONT

1/2" STOCK SIDES AND BACK

1 1/2" SQ. X 12 1/2" LEG STOCK (4)

1" SQ. X 12" SLIDES

1" X 8" LEG BLOCK

tenons on a lathe or whittle them to shape. An easier, but less effective way, is to drill for dowel inserts. To find the center, draw diagonal lines between the corners of the narrower end, drill ¾-inch holes about one inch deep and glue in dowels so that one inch extends for the tenon.

The leg holes are drilled straight into the cleats of the bench top, and the legs are glued in. A bit of adjustment with a wood rasp will be necessary to equalize the leg lengths so the table stands steady.

With this stage completed you have the basic cobbler's bench. The "superstructure" can be added at leisure: the compart-

ment dividers, the planter recess, the rim molding, and the handy drawer slung underneath. Top edges of all partitions are neatly rounded. The drawer has a pair of side runners that fit into rabbeted guides. Keep in mind that the drawer is mounted directly under the single-thickness bench top, so the guide is placed alongside the end cleat.

The planter section at the end comprises two boards, 5 inches high, each of which is grooved near the top for the slide cover.

Finishing is best done with dark maple stain, allowed to penetrate deeply into the wood, followed with wax or shellac coat. •

Key and Letter Rack

Household keys and daily
mail will always be within
reach of all in the family

Hanging wall planter is a reminder to take your keys and
mail those letters. The top
holder is for incoming mail.

The top edges of the letter racks are contoured; lower edges are beveled 30 degrees with a plane.

Glue the beveled edges and nail on from both the front and back, using nails of correct length.

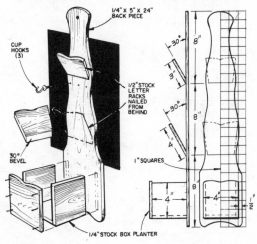

THIS HANDY WALL hanger serves as a constant reminder to take your keys and mail your letters. Located near the vestibule, where its tiny growing plant also offers a cheerful greeting, it has neat racks for incoming and outgoing mail, plus a row of hooks for keys.

It takes only two 2-foot lengths of ¼-inch solid pine board, 5 inches wide. A discarded fruit wood box can supply the needed material.

Draw half the pattern of the back panel on a piece of folded wrapping paper and cut along the outline. When the paper is opened flat, both sides will be uniform. The back should be 24 inches long. It is about 5 inches wide at the lower end and tapers to a rounded top, about 3 inches wide. Notice that the bottom edge is contoured to minimize the appearance of bulk.

Trace the pattern directly on the wood. Cut with a coping saw or jig saw. The plant box sides are 4 by 4 inches; the bottom is 3½ by 4 inches—if the stock is a full ¼ inch in thickness. If not, adjust the

bottom length to fit. The diagram gives all needed dimensions.

Joints are brushed with glue before nailing. Ends of two sides overlap the bottom (on its shorter length), then the front will fit flush with the edges of the sides and bottom. First nail the sides to the bottom, then set vertically so the front can be nailed on. Use headless brads, ½ inch or ⅝ inch long. The open end of the box is centered on the back panel ¾ inch from the bottom, and nailed on through the back.

The two letter holders are strips of the same wood, 3 by 4 inches, fastened to the back at an angle. After these pieces are cut to size and one long edge curved with the coping saw, the bottom edge is beveled (about 30 degrees) with a plane. Fasten with short brads, through the back as well as from the front.

Now shape the top edge of the planter box front to the same design as that on the two letter holders, and drill a small centered hole in the rounded top end of the panel, for hanging on the wall. •

Floor Lamp

Pleasant shaded light and a convenient table in one unit

Colonial-style floor lamp provides perfect light for reading, and a convenient table for books and trays.

THIS COLONIAL bridge lamp is a perfect complement for your favorite reading chair—the double sockets offer good lighting, the ample hexagonal table is convenient for ash trays, books, etc. The lamp is 64 inches high to the top of the bulb sockets; the table is 28 inches above the floor and 20 inches diagonally across the corners.

You'd never guess the source of the gracefully tapered base pedestal—it's fashioned from a discarded baseball bat! This greatly simplifies the project for those who do not have a wood-turning lathe. The beautifully grained hickory blends well with the pine used for the rest of the project.

Start with the pedestal, which, of course, should be solid and sanded smooth. Saw off the bat handle to leave a 21-inch length. The thickness at the handle will be about 1½ inches. With a rasp, turn down this end to form a tenon one inch long and about one inch in diameter. Into the center of

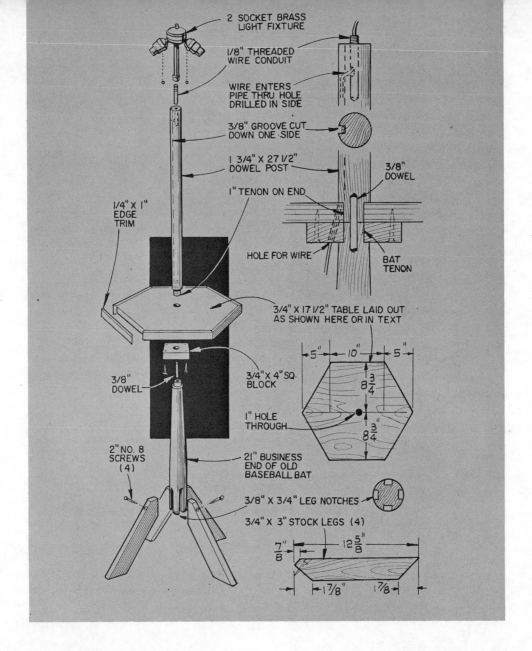

2 SOCKET BRASS
LIGHT FIXTURE

1/8" THREADED
WIRE CONDUIT

WIRE ENTERS
PIPE THRU HOLE
DRILLED IN SIDE

3/8" GROOVE CUT
DOWN ONE SIDE

1 3/4" X 27 1/2"
DOWEL POST

3/8"
DOWEL

1" TENON ON END

1/4" X 1"
EDGE
TRIM

HOLE FOR WIRE

BAT
TENON

3/4" X 17 1/2" TABLE LAID OUT
AS SHOWN HERE OR IN TEXT

3/8"
DOWEL

3/4" X 4" SQ.
BLOCK

1" HOLE
THROUGH

5"   10"   5"

3 3/4

3 3/4

2" NO. 8
SCREWS
(4)

21" BUSINESS
END OF OLD
BASEBALL BAT

3/8" X 3/4" LEG NOTCHES

3/4" X 3" STOCK LEGS (4)

7/8"   12 5/8"

1 7/8"   1 7/8"

this tenon drill a ⅜-inch hole to a depth of one inch for a dowel to connect with and hold the top extension pole. Now saw a plate from ¾-inch plywood to a 4- by 4-inch size. Drill a one-inch hole through the center and fit the tenon into this hole.

The legs are made of clear 1- by 3-inch pine. Cut four pieces to 14-inch lengths. One end of each leg is sawed at a 30-degree angle, the other end at a 45-degree angle in the same direction. At the 30-degree corner, go back two inches from the end

and make a 45-degree cut to chop off the point. The drawing shows how the leg looks with the three angle cuts. Make all four legs the same.

The thick end of the bat is now notched to receive the legs. Cut the notches to a depth of ⅜ of an inch, wide enough to take the legs. You must make a simple jig that will hold the round bat when running it through the saw; a piece of wood tacked to the handle end of the bat will do. Mark the bat so the dado grooves will be equi-

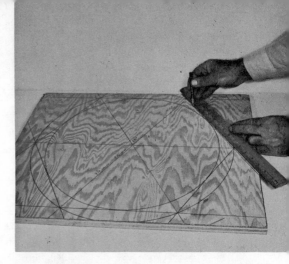

Six-sided table is marked for the cuts. Draw two circles as shown, connect points that intersect outer circle and saw sides. Drill center hole.

Thicker end of bat is notched to ⅜-inch depth for the four legs. Legs are fastened into the notches with glue and long countersunk screws.

A wood plate that holds the bat tenon is attached to the underside of the table with screws. Tenon extends through the square plate into table top.

The top pole is also tenoned to fit the table hole while a center hole permits linking dowel to both top and lower standards. Join with glue.

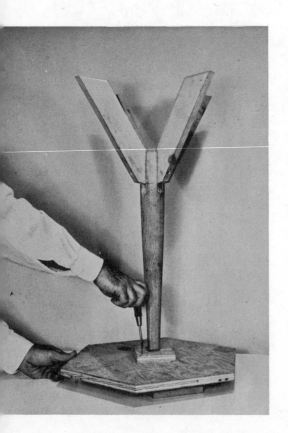

distant all around. Also, clamp a stop gauge to the saw table so the bat will go forward only four inches for each cut. The grooves will be rounded at the top end, adding an interesting effect. Or, you can eliminate this by making the grooves just three inches long and squaring the top end with a chisel. The legs are glued in uniformly, then drilled for deeply countersunk reinforcing screws.

The hexagonal table is next. Use ¾-inch knotty-pine veneered plywood, or join together two pieces of 1- by 10-inch pine boards, 18 inches long. Find the center position and draw two circles, one with an 8½-inch radius, the other with a 9⅞-inch radius. Draw a diameter line through the circles. Draw two additional diameter lines at 60 degrees to the original line. Connect the points where the lines bisect the larger circle. This establishes the six sides of the table. Cut the board on those lines.

Drill a 1-inch center hole and put the table board on the leg assembly. The pedestal plate is attached underneath the table with screws, and the bat tenon should go part way into the table hole.

The top pole is a 1¾-inch dowel, 27½ inches long. Drill a ⅜-inch hole at both ends to a depth of 1½ inches. Now cut a ⅜-inch groove all along the outside of this pole so that the lamp cord can be recessed inside.

With a rasp, turn down one end of the pole to form a tenon to fit into the 1-inch table hole, which, coincidentally, will admit the pedestal dowel. Glue the pole and leg assembly to the table.

The lamp fittings consist of a 7-inch length of ⅛-inch threaded pipe, turned into the top of the pole. Drill a ¼-inch hole at the grooved side of the pole so that the lamp wire can be brought out at the side and held inside the groove with staples. Put a decorative brass turning over the threaded pipe and add double sockets at the top to a special lamp assembly available at all hardware stores. Drill a tiny hole into the table near the pole groove so you can bring the lamp cord through, under the table.

Dress the table edges with strips of mitered trellis stock, ¼ inch thick and finish the lamp with a stain of desired color. •

Lamp fittings consist of threaded pipe that goes deep into pole, and a covering brass tube with double sockets. Lamp cord comes through the side.

The table edge is dressed with one-inch strips of ¼-inch trellis stock, mitered at the corners and attached with casein glue and headless brads.

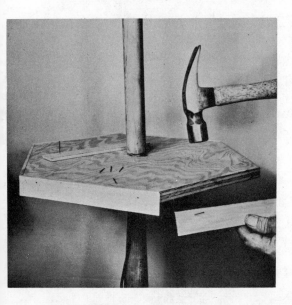

Fireplace Mantel

A darkly stained, country-style mantel lends atmosphere to the home

ROUGH-HEWN, massive fireplace mantels set a charming country atmosphere for the home. Even the knots and gouges in the wood accentuate the glow of burnished pine to form a perfect backdrop for colonial furnishings. There is a modern refinement, however, in the mantel shown. Instead of a solid wood beam which would be of considerable weight and expose splintering end grain, this one is a box with mitered front corners which are casually rounded. The unit is supported by two scroll-cut brackets attached to the wall.

Wood for the box front and sides is select-grade pine, with small and tight knots, designated as 5/4 thickness but actually full one-inch stock. If the mantel is to be six feet long, you'll need a single 8-foot length of board 4 inches wide. This will be enough for the front and the two

Bring warmth of early-type fireplace into your living room to complement your colonial furnishings.

sides. Each side is 8¼ inches deep. For the top and bottom, get two 6-foot lengths of regular 1- by 8-inch stock. The back piece requires a 6-foot length of 2- by 2-inch stock, and the brackets, two feet of 2- by 8-inch clear pine.

For the front and sides, the 4-inch stock is ripped down a bit to 3¾-inch width, though you may prefer to use the full stock width, especially if the mantel is of extra length. Miter both ends of the front piece, and one end of each side.

Rip the 1x8 for the top and bottom pieces, and cut to fit between the sides. A dish groove is cut one inch from the long back edge of the top board. Before assembling, shape the two brackets, following the profile in the drawing.

The front, sides and bottom are joined, using glue and nails. The partially com-

pleted box is attached to the brackets with screws through the bottom board, making sure the parts are flush and square. The back strip is then fitted and nailed in, and the box completed by adding the top board. Fill all nail holes. Stain the mantel box before installation on the wall. A few gouges, made with a small chisel, will add to the attractiveness.

Drill two holes in each bracket, one at the narrowest part and the other just under the top bulge. Attach the brackets above the fireplace with masonry anchors. First drill only one hole, using a carbide-tipped drill of the correct size for the anchor. Turn in the one screw, then level off the mantel and mark for the second screw. When the two screws are in place, the others can be located and drilled. Now comes sanding, polishing, waxing until the pine gleams. •

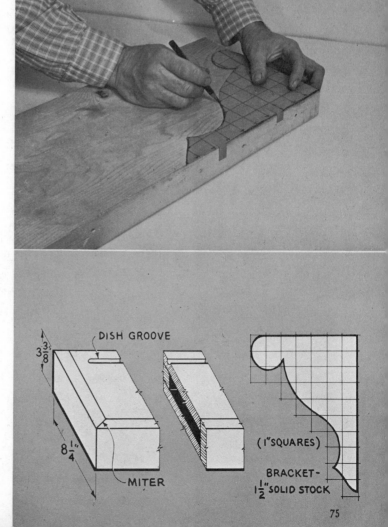

Pattern for the brackets is made on a grid of one-inch squares and traced directly on the clear pine.

Front and sides of extra-heavy stock are mitered, and back strip is fitted between top and bottom.

DISH GROOVE

3⅜

8¼"

MITER

(1"SQUARES)

BRACKET-
1½"SOLID STOCK

Contours of the rough-cut brackets are shaped on a sander and smoothened by filing and sandpapering.

Groove to prevent dishes from falling is cut with a chisel, one inch from back edge of top board.

The front and sides are
attached to bottom and
partially completed box
is attached to brackets.

Top board and back strip
are added last, but sand,
dust and stain assembly
before final installation.

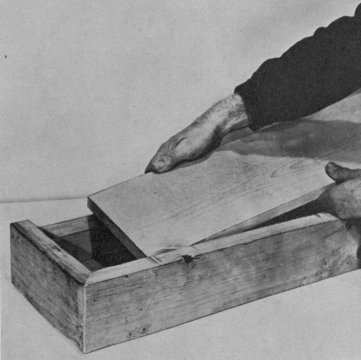

Dry Sink Hutch

The perfect example of traditional furniture, attractive and spacious

COMMODIOUS storage space, traditional proportions, and the gleaming tones of polished pine wood mark this concept of the ever-popular dry sink hutch cabinet. With all its complex details that add so much to this creative new design, the hutch is not a very difficult or extensive project for the serious hobbyist. Actual construction has been quite simplified except for the doors, with their beveled insert panels which may be done on either bench saw or jointer. However, if you want to keep this part of the work in the hand tool category, the doors can be modified by substituting board-and-batten construction.

The simulated peg detail, shown, involves no difficulty as it is merely a means of covering recessed screwheads with short plugs or dowels glued into place.

All needed dimensions are given in the diagram on the next page. It also shows the decorative contours in one-inch squares for duplication. Material used is one-inch knotty pine stock for all except the inside compartment shelves, for which ¾-inch plywood may be used, and the backing

Beautifully grained cabinet has ample storage space for large trays and plates, drawers hold silverware.

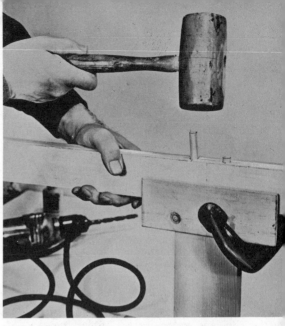

The front frame is assembled with dowels, joining uprights at the ends and wider, center upright.

Use clamped boards to hold members flush. Dowels are driven in and excess trimmed with saw blade.

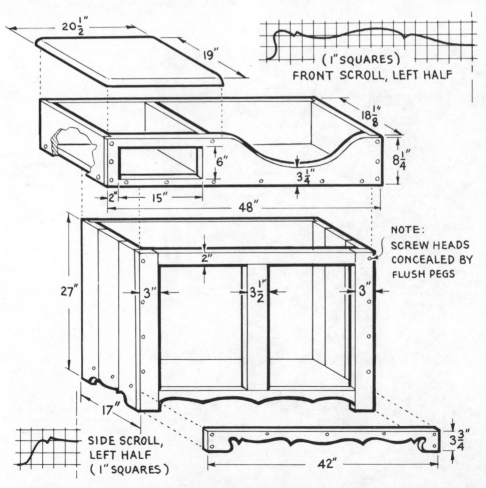

$20\frac{1}{2}$"

19"

(1"SQUARES)
FRONT SCROLL, LEFT HALF

$18\frac{1}{8}$

$8\frac{1}{4}$"

6"

$3\frac{1}{4}$"

2"

15"

48"

NOTE:
SCREW HEADS
CONCEALED BY
FLUSH PEGS

27"

2"

3"

$3\frac{1}{2}$

3"

17"

SIDE SCROLL,
LEFT HALF
(1"SQUARES)

42"

$3\frac{3}{4}$"

panel of ¼-plywood or hardboard. There are only two shallow drawers (each having a pair of white porcelain handles) and these may be made of ¼- or ½-inch solid stock. The compartment base and the overhang top structure are made separately and joined together.

All screw holes are drilled with a Stanley Screwmate which drills the screw pilot holes and also the depth for recessing the screwheads in one operation.

For the base, start by forming the two side panels, made by edge-gluing three random pieces of stock to a total width of 17 inches. Each side is grooved three inches above the bottom to receive the ¾-inch plywood shelf. Also, the rear edges of the sides are rabbeted for the back panel, and the scroll pattern shown is cut into the bottom of each side.

Now the front frame is made as shown, joining the two 3-inch-wide side uprights plus a 3½-inch-wide center upright to the top and bottom cross members. These parts are joined with dowels by drilling through from the outside deep into the joined board and driving in the dowels all the way. The

dowel ends are sawed off flush; the exposed end will look just like the flush plugs covering the screwheads.

The bottom rail of the frame is jigsawed so that it will not show in back of the additional decorative member that goes in front of it. Attach the frame to the sides with recessed screws, insert the shelf into its dado grooves, and nail on the back panel. Cut the front strip 3¾ inches by 42 inches long, make the design from the ruled pattern, and attach with screws along the bottom front. This completes the cabinet base.

For the top section, first form the front board. This is 8¼ by 48 inches. Rabbet both ends for joining the sides of the box. Make the 6-inch-high by 15-inch-wide drawer cutout two inches from the left end, then cut the graceful curve along the top at the other side, starting 20 inches from the left end and finishing just before the rabbet cut at the other end.

The two side pieces are made next, each 8¼ by 18⅛ inches. One end of these boards is rabbeted for the rear side of the box. With these sides and the original front tem-

Join the front frame to the assembled sides and shelf. Notice contoured cuts at bottom end of side piece.

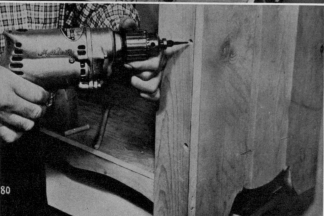

Attach frame by drilling pilot holes with Stanley Screwmate which forms recessed holes for screws.

80

porarily set in place, get the correct length of the back board to fit between the rabbets. Now the front, back and side pieces are dadoed for a ¾-inch plywood bottom. Besides, vertical grooves are cut into the front and back boards for the separator insert which goes 18 inches from the left edge. Assemble the box with its bottom panel and the separator, using screws and nails. A shelf is placed for the drawer support into the drawer section attached to the compartment boards.

Finally, the top panel, 19 by 20½ inches, is cut and the edges slightly beveled or rounded. Attach with headless nails to the dry sink compartment.

Make the drawer, with facings of the same stock, each just high enough to fit the opening above and below the shelf support drawer. Complete the drawers with simple rabbet corners and nailed-in bottoms.

Now use dowel lengths, or short plugs cut on a drill press, to fill the screw pilot holes for the pegged effect. Glue the dowels into place, then cut off flush with a hacksaw blade removed from its frame. •

The screwheads are driven as deep as possible to leave space for the decorative dowel "pegs."

Use special light maple plugs to offer contrast to dark pine since hardwood does not take the stain.

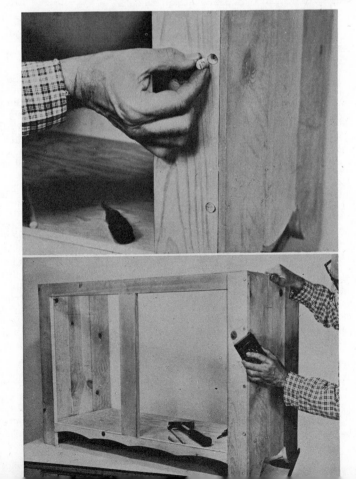

Round off corners to reduce heavy look. Bottom cabinet now is ready for decorative scroll facing.

Handy Wall Case

Undoubtedly an adaptation, but it does make a decorative piece

Unusual design of a stained pine wall case makes a graceful showpiece in a Colonial-style home.

I T WOULD BE DIFFICULT to find an explanation for this old fruitwood case, the original of which was encountered in a small antique shop. The lid pivots at the back to fold down on the top shelf, indicating that perhaps it was intended for a stool. But then, what is the purpose of the bottom drawer and side finger slots?

Actually, no justification is needed beyond the fact that a simplified version makes it a graceful and interesting wall case for small plants and bric-a-brac that will complement any Early American room. The extra drawer also will be found useful as a special hideaway spot.

The unit can be readily made from any ¼-inch stock, though heavier ½-inch clear pine board should be obtained for the sides. The drawings give adequate data for cutting and assembling the parts.

The sides are important, as the unusual contour of the exposed edges lends the essential "hand-wrought" tone to the piece. Each side is cut from a ½-inch-thick board at least 7½ by 14 inches. Copy the design for the sides from the drawing on heavy paper. Make half the outline, then fold the paper and cut along the lines to complete the pattern since both the top and bottom sections of the sides are identical. Transfer the pattern directly on the wood.

Both sides can be cut at the same time by nailing them together temporarily on the waste side of the stock. Use a jig or band saw, or cut with a coping saw. Mark and drill the finger-grip slots in the sides.

All the other parts, except the drawer front, are cut from ¼-inch solid pine board. Cut two shelves, each 6 by 15 inches, and the back panel, 11 by 15 inches.

Assemble the parts you already have, because the others must be closely fitted into place. Nail the back panel to the shelves so they are flush with the top and bottom edges of the panel, then attach the sides so they extend equally at top and bottom, about 1½ inches at each end.

Now cut the vertical divider, 6 inches wide, and about 10½ inches long, adjusting the length dimension so that the divider fits snugly between the shelves. Take care also that the ends of this divider are square so they will match the shelves to which

they are joined with nails through the top and bottom shelves.

The next two parts are the horizontal and vertical dividers for the small right-hand section, 6¼ inches wide on the inside, as shown in the drawings.

A ¾-inch-wide band, such as trellis stock, is notched at the ends as shown, glued and nailed to the front edge of the top shelf. The lid, strangely, is framed on three sides with narrow stock; this most likely was done to give a better anchor for the pivot pins which are nails driven through each of the sides. The ends of the frame are slightly rounded with a file.

The lid must be positioned slightly above the shelf for clearance when it turns on the pivots. A uniform clearance is obtained by laying a strip of cardboard under the lid while the nails are driven in.

The drawer is of the simplest construction consisting of a ½-inch-thick front with rabbet cuts to which the drawer sides and bottom are nailed, and the back is also fastened with nails to the sides and bottom. The drawer front overlaps the frame by ⅛ inch on each side.

Make sure the wood has been carefully sanded before assembling. Apply penetrat-

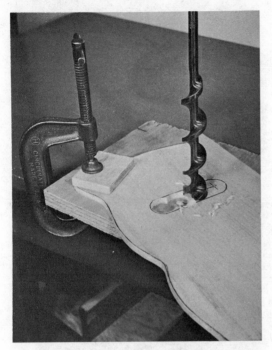

Finger-grip slots in sides are cut by drilling with an auger bit and filing the inside edges.

ing oil stain of the desired shade, wipe off the excess after a few minutes and rub with a padded cloth until the surface is dry.

After a coat of shellac, or just an application of wax, the case is ready to be hung on the wall by means of standard metal flat hangers. •

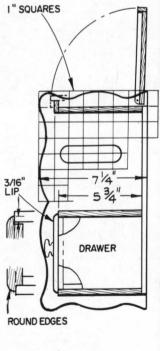

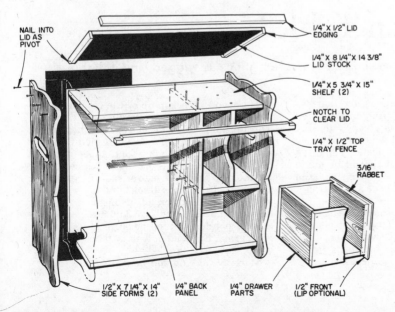

Lazy Susan Table

Easy to make, charming conversation piece is rugged and reliable

BURNISHED to a lustrous gloss that belies its ruggedness, the handicrafted pine Lazy Susan table is steeped in tradition and loved by all who build their homes around Early American styling. It's the kind of furniture that should be made and polished at home. The cost is little, the gratification very great. There are no tricky joints or fancy hardware.

Doweling is the chief process in the construction, so you should have, or get, an inexpensive doweling jig with a ⅜-inch guide barrel. A brace and bit and a jig or portable saber saw are also necessary.

The wood used is pine of the No. 2 common grade having some small, tight knots. The top may be made of regular shelving boards which are only about ¾ inch thick, but if you prefer a more solid appearance, buy what is known as 5/4 stock, which will be fine also for the base rails. The legs are shown as 1½ inches thick, but there, too, you have the option of using somewhat heavier lumber, up to 2 by 2 inches, preferably of ponderosa pine because of its uniform grain. Exposed dowels will be of birch wood.

Start by making the base. Cut the four

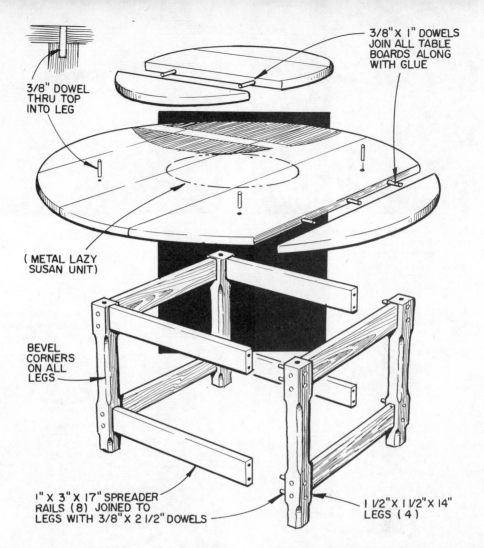

3/8" X 1" DOWELS JOIN ALL TABLE BOARDS ALONG WITH GLUE

3/8" DOWEL THRU TOP INTO LEG

(METAL LAZY SUSAN UNIT)

BEVEL CORNERS ON ALL LEGS

1" X 3" X 17" SPREADER RAILS (8) JOINED TO LEGS WITH 3/8" X 2 1/2" DOWELS

1 1/2" X 1 1/2" X 14" LEGS (4)

Drawing shows details of how the sections are assembled with dowels and glue. Photos show how legs and sides are carefully clamped and glued, then drilled and doweled while clamps are still in place. Note boards under side pieces which raise them to a proper and uniform height before clamping—and provide further support while the holes for dowels are being drilled. When first side is done, repeat process as shown at right.

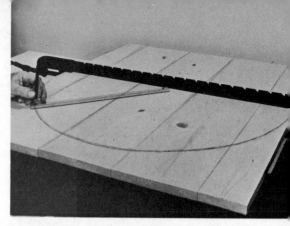

When glued sections are thoroughly dry, ends of dowels are cut off with hacksaw blade. Now the corners can be chamfered with a spokeshave.

Select pieces for top, clamp together and then draw your circle. Take apart again and mark and drill for dowels. Draw new circle after assembly.

Hole positions are marked on adjacent boards for correct alignment of the dowels. Dowling jig is necessary for positive alignment of dowel holes.

After the boards are doweled together draw fresh circle line and cut along this line with jig saw or band saw. Drawing shows placement of dowels.

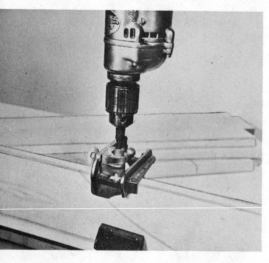

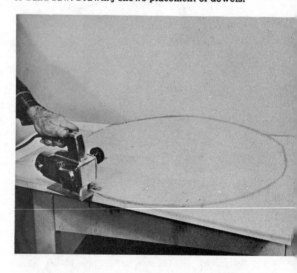

legs 14 inches long, and eight 1- by 3-inch rails, approximately 18 inches long, depending on the thickness of the leg stock, but all of uniform size. The legs are first jointed with dowels to the rails in pairs, then assembled to a square base by adding the other rails. The doweling will go quickly if you follow this procedure:

Mark center lines on two surfaces of the legs, near the top and bottom. Cut a few pieces of scrap wood that, when placed under the rails, will hold them centered to the leg thickness. These "spacers" should be of a thickness so that two of them plus the rail will be exactly equal to the thickness of the leg stock.

Place two legs on the bench, set a rail across two or more spacers so they are flush with the leg ends, and another rail 2 inches from the other ends. Tighten a pipe clamp across the legs, then drill two $\frac{3}{8}$-inch holes at each end straight through the legs and to a depth of at least one inch into the rails. Dip the dowels into glue and drive them into the holes. Cut off projecting ends of the dowel with a hacksaw blade, and sand smooth. Repeat the process, but altering the dowel positions, to join the two pairs of legs with the rails to make the square base.

The top is built up of random boards to about 32-inch width. Clamp the boards together, draw the circle with a stick pivoting

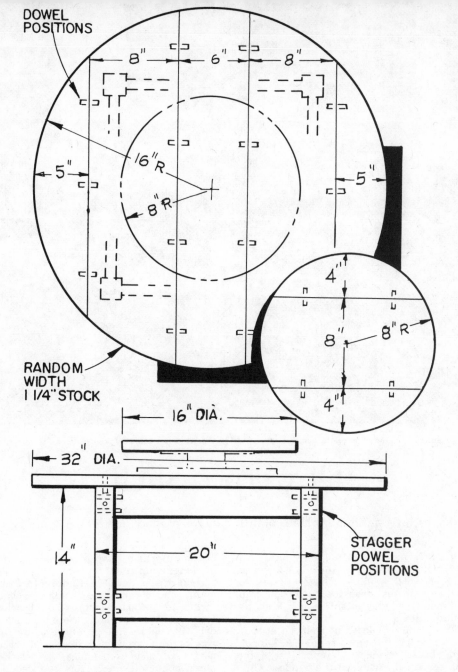

DOWEL POSITIONS

8"   6"   8"

16"R

8"R

5"   5"

RANDOM
WIDTH
1 1/4" STOCK

4"

8"   8"R

4"

16" DIA.

32" DIA.

14"   20"

STAGGER
DOWEL
POSITIONS

on a center nail, mark and number the dowel positions across the boards where they will be joined. With the doweling jig, drill holes and join the boards together with dowels and glued edges. Cut out the circle with a jig or saber saw.

The top is also attached to the base with dowels, a single dowel into each leg. This is done by holding the top in position and drilling right through. Drive each dowel down flush with the top surface, as it will be difficult to saw off the dowel end with-

out damaging the top. The birch dowel will contrast nicely with the stained pine.

The Lazy Susan tray is made of glued-up pieces, fitted on a standard metal revolving fixture available at most lumber and craft supply houses at about a dollar.

The final step before finishing is to chamfer the leg corners with a spokeshave, and to round the rail edges slightly. A few dents will add to the appearance. Finish with stain, thin coats of pumice-rubbed shellac, and well-rubbed wax. •

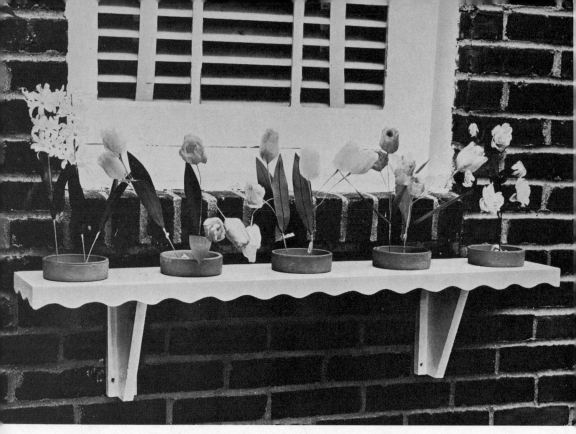

Simple rack holds flowers in colorful array outside the window; can be taken in on colder days.

Flowerpot Shelf

Even in late autumn potted plants can be placed out in the midday sun

WHEN you take in the geraniums this fall set them out in the sun whenever there is good weather. The easy way to do this is to just drop the flowerpots into this handy window planter rack with its round cutouts.

The planter rack is, in itself, an attractive ornament for any window. A 7-inch-wide board is cut to length, just a bit longer than the width of the window. Circles of 4-inch diameter for standard size flowerpots are cut with a jig or coping saw.

The support brackets are made in this way: Rip a piece of 1-inch shelving lumber to 7-inch width. Cut off an 8½-inch length. Mark off 5¼ inches from the edge, on one end, and mark the 1¾-inch position from that same edge on the other end. Draw a line between the two points. Sawing along this diagonal line will give you two pieces of lumber, 8½ inches long, 5¼ inches wide at one end, 1¾ inches wide

at the other end. Two brackets will serve for lengths up to 40 inches.

Next rip a piece of lumber to 2-inch width, and cut off two lengths, each 8½ inches, for the back plates of the brackets. Draw a center line along these back pieces, drill three holes in each for attaching with screws to the straight edge of each bracket part. Drill also four holes in each back plate, about one inch from top and bottom on each side. These holes are for fastening the brackets to the wall under your window. But the brackets are fastened to the flower rack with wood screws from the top.

The rack is now trimmed along the front and sides with 1½-inch-wide strips of scalloped molding cut from ¼-inch trellis stock. You can buy this ready-cut decorative trim at any lumberyard, or cut your own on a jig or band saw. Nail the strips to the front and sides of your

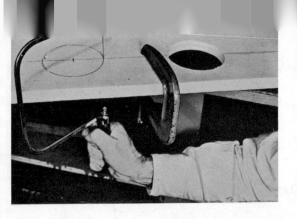

If coping saw doesn't clear the entire circumference, pull blade out and set up on opposite side.

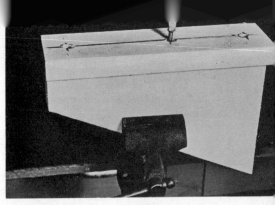

The wall brackets, with sloped front, are made in two parts, joined with screws through the back.

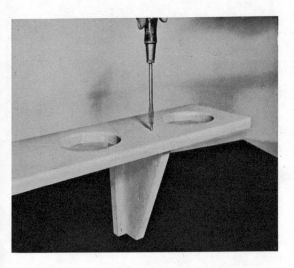

Attach the rack directly to bracket with screws. Drill pilot holes to prevent splitting the wood.

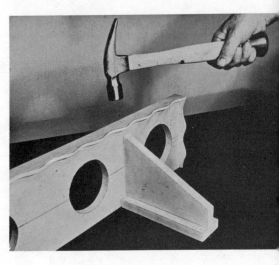

Decorative molding can be cut out at home, or the scalloped wood trim can be bought at lumberyard.

flower rack with headless brads. Paint the entire unit with two coats of exterior-grade paint in desired color.

Attaching the brackets under the window to a wood siding or shingle wall is easy enough, involving just eight wood screws turned tightly into the wall. To fasten the brackets on brick, stucco and fieldstone walls, drill holes for masonry anchors. Fiber Rawlplug anchors are suitable for this purpose as they won't deteriorate from rain and the elements, will hold the flower rack securely for an indefinite period. Another advantage is that only very small holes are needed, and these can be pointed up easily if the rack is removed at some later date.

Drill a ¼-inch hole, using a carbide-tipped bit in an electric drill, or a No. 12 percussion star drill if the work is done by hand. Drill the holes straight and only to a depth that will receive the length of the fiber plug, which is about 1½ inches. Push in the lead-center plug, set the bracket in place and turn on a No. 12 wood screw, two inches long.

Mark the positions for the next holes, remove the bracket by turning out the first screw so you can continue with the rest of the drilling and the holes will line up with the bracket holes. The important detail is that the drill, Rawlplugs and the wood screws must be the same size—all No. 12 for safe anchorage. •

Knotty Pine Breakfront

Fill in an unneeded doorway and put in a practical piece of furniture

Knotty pine boards make planked background for breakfront built into a wall having a shallow jog.

ONE OF THE attributes of tongue-and-groove knotty pine is that it is easy to work, even for making large cabinets. The boards are joined wherever necessary without the intricate fitting required for plywood projects. Profiled designs milled along the edges on one side of the board and simple "V" bevels on the reverse side offer flexibility and variety of arrangement, have the appearance of planks. Nailheads are easily concealed because of the grain figures. Properly cured wood, when preconditioned to room temperatures and atmosphere, is quite stable; the tongue-and-groove joints allow for expansion with sufficient tolerance. While quite soft and

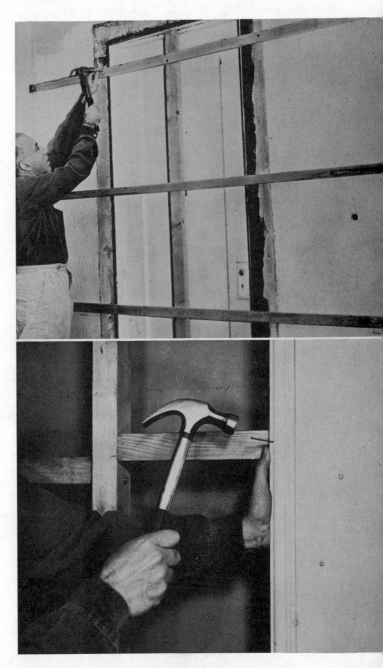

The wall is prepared with horizontal furring strips nailed through the plaster into original wall studs.

Blind nailing through the tongues makes perfect assembly. Nailheads will be hidden by adjoining board.

easy to saw, knotty pine has a rich beauty when stained and rubbed.

The built-in breakfront shown covers a section of wall that formerly was a doorway. Instead of replastering, the opening was finished with 1- by 8-inch Idaho white pine boards over horizontal furring strips nailed to the old studs.

These wall planks, arranged with the plain "V" edges showing, serve as a background for shallow shelves, to hold a collection of pewter and brassware, as part of a breakfront. The shelves are held in dado grooves cut into the side uprights that rest on the lower cabinet. The same boards are reversed for the lower buffet, showing their milled design. Standing 36

inches high, 18 inches deep, the cabinet is framed and built right at the wall. The installation shown was built in a shallow alcove.

The construction starts with three 2-inch strips nailed directly to the planked background. One strip is at floor level, the second is at the desired height for the middle shelf, the third strip will support the buffet counter, so is 36 inches above the floor.

The sides are 18 inches wide, formed of boards cut 36 inches long, joined with 1- by 2-inch battens across the back. These are located to match the three original strips across the back wall.

The front frame is now formed, consist-

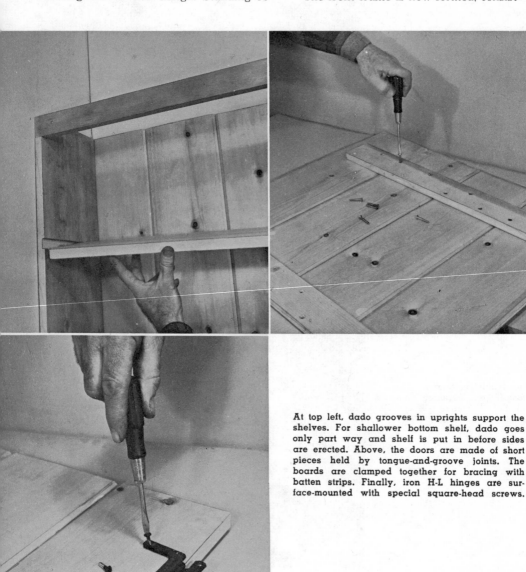

At top left, dado grooves in uprights support the shelves. For shallower bottom shelf, dado goes only part way and shelf is put in before sides are erected. Above, the doors are made of short pieces held by tongue-and-groove joints. The boards are clamped together for bracing with batten strips. Finally, iron H-L hinges are surface-mounted with special square-head screws.

ing of a 2-inch-wide strip full length for the bottom, two uprights ripped 4 inches wide for the ends, a top horizontal member 3 inches wide, and a center divider upright. The ends that are to be joined to the sides should be cut so the milled design fits into the corner after the tongues are ripped off. If the unit is to go against an end wall, as in the one shown in the photographs, then one of the uprights should be jigsawed to fit the contours of the base moldings, starting two inches above the floor. When the parts are ready, arrange them flat on the floor, join the corners temporarily with corrugated fasteners at the back.

Stand the frame in position, nail the sides to the end uprights. Put in the bottom shelf so it rests on, and fits flush, with the bottom strip, cutting the front corners to clear the end uprights. Notch for a center divider at the front, and an inside shelf partition if desired.

The top may be of two solid boards, edge-glued together to obtain the needed 18-inch width so the top edges overlay the cabinet frame ½ inch at front and sides. If ¾-inch pine-veneered plywood is used, dress the exposed edges with veneer strips or ¼-inch wood bands.

Doors are made of the same pine stock, joined with battens attached with screws across the back, and fitted with black iron hinges and latches. •

The spacious buffet cabinet provides space for a complete audio system including an enclosed TV set.

Cranberry Scoop

An early-day tool made for use in a conventional home

A tool used in gathering cranberries scores with modern homemakers who value its interesting design and the heritage of Early American products.

THE CRANBERRY scoop typifies a functional work tool of such interesting form that it has been adapted to many uses in the home. In various sizes, but retaining the overall proportions for decorative values, it is used as a wall planter, magazine rack, notebook holder, even as a rack for pot covers and trays.

The ingenious hand-wrought scoop is a memento of the early-day method for gathering the cranberry crop from almost impenetrable bramble shrubs which grow in low bogs. The marshy fields are diked and flooded so that men in flat-bottom boats can thresh the bushes with sticks. The berries fall into the water where they float and can be scooped up. The slatted end of the scoop, like the tines of a fork, retain the berries while permitting the water to drain off.

If you want to make a cranberry scoop for your own home, the first step is to obtain some clear pine board of actual ½- or ⅝-inch thickness.

The drawings show the dimensions for each of the parts needed to duplicate the scoop shown. The only problem is that you will need an extra-wide piece into which the prongs are cut. Occasionally lumber dealers have 15″ widths in stock, but if necessary you can edge-glue two boards to get the required 13⅝-inch width.

Make sure when gluing the boards that their faces are perfectly flush, because the side pressure of the clamps tends to pull them out of line. The way to control this is to glue the boards on a flat surface such as a table, which will permit application of additional clamps above the joint as well as from the sides.

Cover the table with waxed paper for a glue barrier. Place the boards together with their best side up. Brush glue on the jointing edge, apply slight pressure with pipe clamps from the sides. Wipe off the squeezed-out glue with a damp cloth, then cover with waxed paper and place a board over the joint. Clamp down on the cover board before tightening the side clamps.

Prongs are cut into this board, about ⅝ inch wide, separated by the width of a saw kerf. In order to do this on a circular

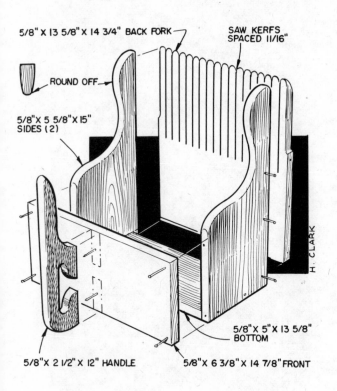

5/8" X 13 5/8" X 14 3/4" BACK FORK

SAW KERFS SPACED 11/16"

ROUND OFF

5/8" X 5 5/8" X 15" SIDES (2)

5/8" X 5" X 13 5/8" BOTTOM

5/8" X 2 1/2" X 12" HANDLE

5/8" X 6 3/8" X 14 7/8" FRONT

H. CLARK

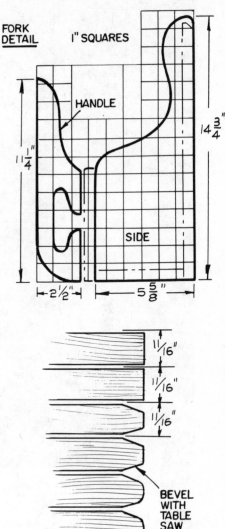

FORK DETAIL

1" SQUARES

HANDLE

11 1/4"

14 3/4"

SIDE

2 1/2"

5 5/8"

11/16"

11/16"

11/16"

BEVEL WITH TABLE SAW THEN FILE ROUND

BEVEL TOP REAR BEFORE SLITTING

saw so all the prongs are uniform, follow this method:

Make the first cut one inch from the end, cutting only to a length of 5 inches. Leave the board with the blade in the kerf. Clamp a stop at that position along the back of the saw table.

Now to adjust the fence for the series of prong cuts. Move the fence away, place a scrap piece of ¾-inch plywood against the edge of the board, then lock the fence against it. Take away the spacer, move the board edge against the fence and run it through for the second cut. Repeating this process will complete the row of uniform prongs, except for the ends which are trimmed down to width by shaping the edges as shown.

The circular saw cuts will be rounded in the inside, so must be squared off with a hand saw, but check to see that the kerf of this saw is not wider than that of the circular blade.

The handle has an interesting design which is copied by making a cardboard pattern and outlining it directly on the wood for shaping with a band saw or hand saber saw. Round off the handle edges with a wood rasp, attach with screws from the back of the board.

The rest is a matter of assembly with counterset one-inch brads, packing the nailholes with putty, and finishing to the desired shade with penetrating oil stain. •

Traditional scroll-cut shelves in oak or maple will make prized pieces part of home decoration.

Colonial Dish Shelves

A style that harmonizes with cherished porcelains and decorative articles

YOUR CHERISHED porcelains and decorated dishes deserve a fitting showcase. This interesting wall shelf will serve this purpose most handsomely.

This type of wall shelf, among the most popular items for homes furnished in one of the Early American periods, is adaptable to almost unlimited variations to suit both personal taste and the purpose for which it is intended. When used above a cabinet or chest of drawers, the width should be modified for a pleasing proportion in relation to the cabinet with which it forms a

room grouping. More or fewer shelves can be used, spaced for your particular collection of bric-a-brac. (See a variation photo and drawing on page 99.) Though you may vary the curved design of the scroll-cut sides for "one-of-a-kind" individuality, the unit retains the unmistakable quality of its rustic Early American source.

Cost of the lumber required is nominal, and in many cases enough small scrap pieces will be found to do the project. A single 3-foot length of 1- by 10-inch board will be sufficient for cutting both side

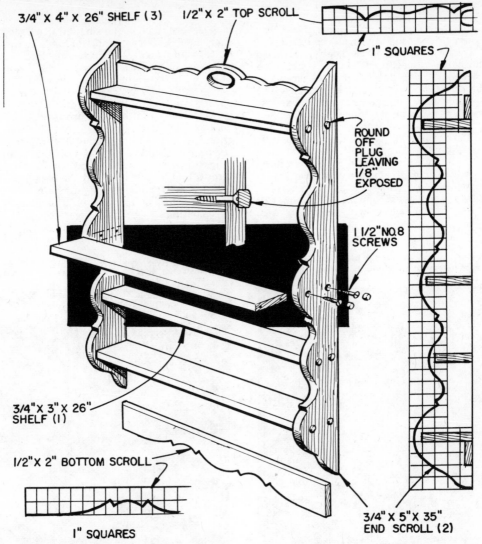

3/4" X 4" X 26" SHELF (3)

1/2" X 2" TOP SCROLL

1" SQUARES

ROUND OFF PLUG LEAVING 1/8" EXPOSED

1 1/2" NO.8 SCREWS

3/4" X 3" X 26" SHELF (1)

1/2" X 2" BOTTOM SCROLL

1" SQUARES

3/4" X 5" X 35" END SCROLL (2)

pieces. Top and bottom rails are two inches wide, of the same one-inch stock.

Plain shelving stock is used, preferably with a few small knots, but without pitch streaks or other blemishes. The shelves may be either ½-inch or 1-inch stock. About five feet of 8-inch-wide board will be needed.

Make patterns of the sides and rails, from the diagram, on ruled kraft paper. Outline the pattern directly on the 3-foot-long board for the sides. First arrange the pattern along one edge of the board and trace the outline. Then turn the pattern over, align the straight side with the opposite edge of the board and trace the outline again. Cut along the lines with a jig saw, or a coping saw. When scroll cutting is completed, clamp both sides together in a vise and sandpaper the edges smooth. Use a rasp to smooth down rough or irregular

spots. A piece of sandpaper wrapped around a length of broomstick dowel will be handy for getting into the rounded edges.

Next lay the sides on the bench with the straight edges together, and rule lines across where the shelves will be placed. Use a try square, drawing double lines spaced the thickness of the shelf boards. Drill two holes in each side at the shelf positions; first drill all the way through with a ⅛-inch bit, then turn the boards over and drill to half the thickness of the side with a ¼-inch bit, in the same holes. This is to provide a countersunk recess for the dowel plugs which will cover the shelf screws. Thus the ruled lines are on the inside of the boards covered by the shelves, while the plugs will go on the outside.

Next, the top and bottom rails are cut to the same length as the shelves and shaped according to pattern. Assemble these rails to the sides with tiny, headless brads.

Then, place one of the shelves between the sides, lining it up with the double ruled lines, and drive one-inch No. 8 screws in the countersink holes, at both sides. The unit will hold together, now, so the rest of the shelves can be assembled. Plan the shelf arrangement so that one shelf rests on the bottom cross-rail while the top shelf is directly under the top rail. The front edge of the shelves should be slightly chamfered or beveled to give them a thinner, more pleasing line.

Now the "pegs" can be glued in. Cut pieces of ¼-inch dowel, about ½ inch long, and round one end smoothly (a dowel sharpener, which costs about $1 will do this quickly and neatly). Brush glue into the countersunk holes and drive in the dowel plugs with the rounded end outward.

The shelf cabinet is mounted securely on the wall with two roundhead screws in both top and bottom cross-rails. If wall is of plaster, try to locate the wall studs so the screws have a firm grip. If you can't find the studs, use fiber wall plugs or other masonry fasteners, using screws long enough to hold the weight.

Finish with a penetrating oil stain in the desired color, and follow with shellac or wax coating. •

Use a cut end of an old broomstick faced with sandpaper to round smooth the curved side pieces.

Draw lines across both sides simultaneously for shelf positions, spaced the thickness of lumber.

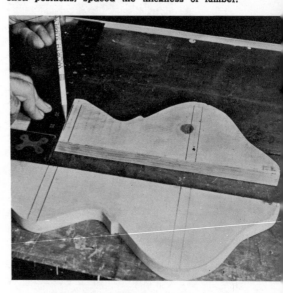

Drill along center lines; turn over to countersink holes to hide screws and receive peg dowels.

Start assembling shelves with screws through the holes in the sides. Turn in No. 8 screws all the way.

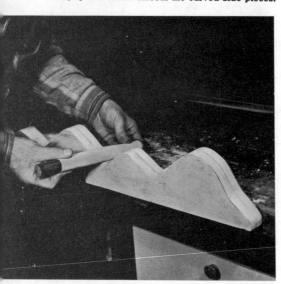

Short piece of dowels are inserted into counter-sunk holes so they project slightly from sides.

Variations of this wall shelf are unlimited, as shown above and below, for smaller bric-a-brac.

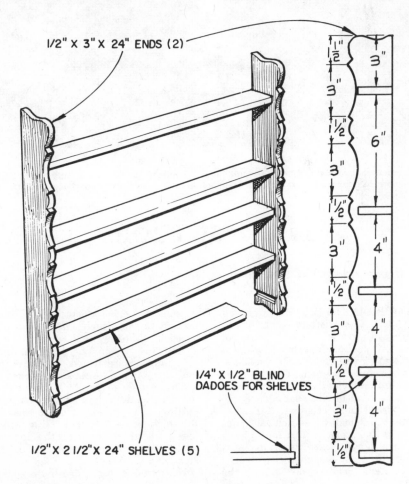

1/2" X 3" X 24" ENDS (2)

1/4" X 1/2" BLIND
DADOES FOR SHELVES

1/2" X 2 1/2" X 24" SHELVES (5)

1 1/2"

3"

3"

1 1/2"

3"

6"

3"

1 1/2"

3"

4"

1 1/2"

3"

4"

1 1/2"

3"

4"

1 1/2"

Beautiful, practical, and imbued with the traditional simplicity of old-time country construction, this distinctive piece of furniture is sturdily built to permit greatest comfort with maximum seating capacity.

Harvest Table

Ideal for use indoors at a summer cottage, or out in a covered terrace

FOR YOUR DINING ROOM or den you may want this distinctive table of ample size, with graceful bright lines, yet of sturdy construction. The table, with its two drop leaves, will comfortably seat ten people when fully opened. The "X"-leg construction is sufficiently rigid to prevent rocking, and won't hinder seating.

The legs are of knot-free, select, straight-grain pine, full 2-inch by 4-inch size (not the ordinary 2x4 stock). Cut four pieces to 34½-inch lengths, set them in pairs forming an "X," just 20 inches apart at the outside corners. Scribe lines across the

outside corners for cutting the top and bottom angles, which will be about 10 degrees, so that they will square.

With the legs in "X" position, mark inside lines where boards cross for cutting half-lap joints. The laps are recessed with a dado set on a circular saw, or done by hand in a miter box with a backsaw by cutting away excess stock to exactly half the thickness of the stock. Glue up the two leg pairs, then chamfer the leg corners with a spokeshave or plane, for a more slender appearance.

Next step is to mortise the leg ends into

Legs are joined in pairs with half-lap joints at the center, ends squared across for mortise-and-tenon joints.

After each pair of legs are joined, tenons are marked and the mortise lines are indexed on mount boards.

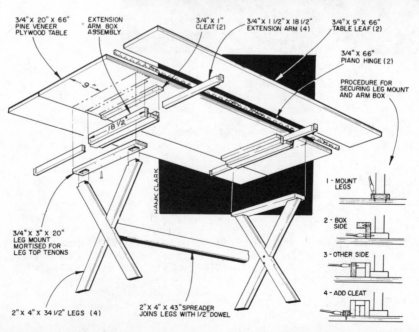

3/4" X 20" X 66" PINE VENEER PLYWOOD TABLE

EXTENSION ARM BOX ASSEMBLY

3/4" X 1" CLEAT (2)

3/4" X 1 1/2" X 18 1/2" EXTENSION ARM (4)

3/4" X 9" X 66" TABLE LEAF (2)

3/4" X 66" PIANO HINGE (2)

PROCEDURE FOR SECURING LEG MOUNT AND ARM BOX

9"

18 1/2

HANK CLARK

3/4" X 3" X 20" LEG MOUNT MORTISED FOR LEG TOP TENONS

2" X 4" X 34 1/2" LEGS (4)

2" X 4" X 43" SPREADER JOINS LEGS WITH 1/2" DOWEL

1 - MOUNT LEGS

2 - BOX SIDE

3 - OTHER SIDE

4 - ADD CLEAT

¾-inch-thick top plates which will secure them to the table top. Each plate is 5 inches wide, 20 inches long. Leg tenons are ¾ inch long, the positions for their opposing mortises are marked along the center of the plates by actual positioning contact. Use a sharp chisel to cut the mortises clear through the plates for a tight fit. Glue the cross legs together.

The legs are reinforced with a 1¼- by 4-inch center stretcher, 48 inches long, joined with two blind dowels at each leg pair. Mark the actual thickness of the stretcher at the leg position, using an angle divider to locate the centers for the dowels, and drill for ⅝-inch dowels. Join the dowel joints with glue to complete the leg assembly.

The table top consists of a ¾-inch plywood panel, 20 inches wide and 6 feet long. Use either knotty pine veneered plywood, or fir with plastic surface laminate. Two drop leaves, each 10 inches wide, are mounted with piano hinges along the ends. The hinge butt faces toward the bottom, and the panel edges are rabbeted somewhat along the bottom edge to recess the hinge so it is not visible when the leaves are raised.

The drop-leaf brackets consist of pull-out bars made of ¾-inch pine, sliding freely in box-like supports. The open-end boxes are secured to the edges of the leg plates, and to cleats at the other sides. A thin wedge on each drop leaf complements the slide-out bar. •

Stretcher joins the leg pairs together, attached at both ends with dowels to give the table solid construction.

Completed assembly of the table shows the placement of parts, with table-leaf slide supports at each end.

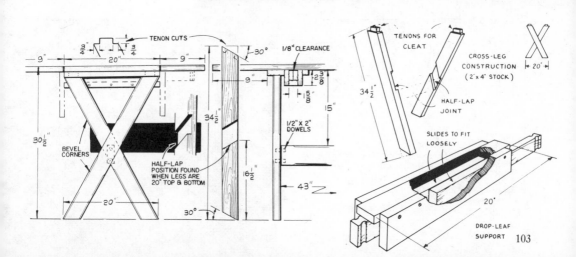

TENON CUTS

¾" ¾"

9" 20" 9"

30° 1/8" CLEARANCE

9"

30½"

BEVEL CORNERS

HALF-LAP POSITION FOUND WHEN LEGS ARE 20" TOP & BOTTOM

20"

34½"

30°

16½"

43"

½" X 2" DOWELS

15"

TENONS FOR CLEAT

34½"

CROSS-LEG CONSTRUCTION (2" x 4" STOCK)

20"

HALF-LAP JOINT

SLIDES TO FIT LOOSELY

20"

DROP-LEAF SUPPORT

A unique variation of this wall rack has three shelves of different shapes to give better display to figurines.

Corner Showcase

Make a colorful setting for your treasured porcelains and objects d'art

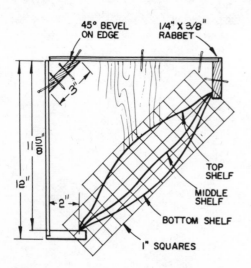

45° BEVEL ON EDGE

1/4" X 3/8" RABBET

3"

11 5/8"

12"

2"

TOP SHELF

MIDDLE SHELF

BOTTOM SHELF

1" SQUARES

Shelves are nailed to the scroll-cut sides and fitted back piece. Sand the edges for finishing.

THOSE always-favorite "what-not" shelves are represented in every furniture period. Because they are basic in style, corner shelves offer a medium for unlimited variations. The unit shown has the particular attraction of extended profile edges that accentuate the texture and grain of the wood.

The shelves and supports are of ½-inch-thick solid wood; the side panels are of ¼-inch solid stock or veneered plywood. A 4-foot piece of ¼-inch material and a 5-foot length of ½-inch wood, both 11¾ inches wide, will be enough for the entire project.

The drawings show dimensions and contours of each part. The three shelves are of the same general width, but note that each is shaped differently at the front edge. The lower shelf is rounded outward, while each other shelf is cut back beyond the last. The topmost shelf is smaller than the rest. The purpose is to enlarge the view so that the pieces on the lower shelves are not overshadowed.

Start by cutting the rear shelf support, 27¾ inches long. The width is 3⅛ inches at the front, but each side is beveled by running it through the saw blade which is tilted at 45 degrees.

The side supports are cut to 25½-inch length, with a ¼- by ¼-inch rabbet along opposing inside edges to recess the side panels. Make a pattern of each part—the rear and side supports, and each shelf—on heavy kraft paper by following the ruled outlines of 1-inch squares. Then trace the patterns directly on the wood and cut the contours with either band or jig saw, a portable bayonet saw, or a simple hand coping saw.

For assembly, place the bottom shelf four inches from the very end of the support and nail it in from the back. The sides are located so the projecting knobs of their profile match the position of this first shelf. The other shelves then are placed to conform with the positions indicated on the side pieces, and are attached with glue and thin brads. The separations between each shelf will be different.

With the shelves securely attached, the side panels are cut to span the space between the side rabbet recesses and the inside wall corner, going well past the bevels of the back supports, but not so far that the panels fail to clear each other into the corner. The unit must fit flush with the corner walls. These panels, glued and nailed at all points to the shelves, sides and back supports, help make the shelf unit solid and secure.

Attach a large metal ring at the back center, and one at each of the sides for hanging on heavy-duty picture hooks so the shelf unit will be safely supported. •

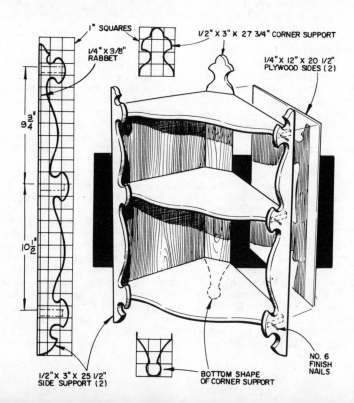

1" SQUARES

¼" X 3/8" RABBET

½" X 3" X 27 3/4" CORNER SUPPORT

¼" X 12" X 20 1/2" PLYWOOD SIDES (2)

9¾"

10½"

½" X 3" X 25 1/2" SIDE SUPPORT (2)

BOTTOM SHAPE OF CORNER SUPPORT

NO. 6 FINISH NAILS

Nail-Box Lamp

A handy light with compartments to hold readily needed articles

IDEAL for the study room or den, this pleasant lamp is in the tradition of our Early American adaptations. The compartments are used for small plants, or to keep needed articles conveniently near the reading chair.

The exceedingly simple construction makes an ideal woodworking project for a young boy, or the novice who hasn't much in the way of tools or experience. There are no tricky joints or fittings, just a few parts to cut to size and nail together and a few holes to drill.

The entire project is made from a 3-foot length of 1- by 9-inch board, and the lamp stem assembly can be bought at any hardware or 5 and 10 store.

The first step is the important one, that of cutting the base 8 inches by 15 inches. It is essential that this be perfectly square. Then cut the two ends, 2¾ by 8 inches, and attach them by nailing through the bottom board. The long sides are next, also 2¾-inch wide, but 13½ inches long, and fit in between the ends for square corner joints.

The centerboard starts as an oblong, 5¾ inches wide by 13½ inches long. This receives two angle cuts as shown in the drawing, done this way: Mark off positions three inches from the corner on both narrow sides, and mark off four inches from the same corner on the long sides. Draw a line between the two points on each side. Saw along the lines to form the angles.

On the same wide board, cut two oval holes, as shown in the drawing, about 1 in. x 2 in., using an ordinary keyhole saw or an electric saber saw. At the center of the top edge drill a ⅜-inch hole with an auger bit, all the way through. Another hole, ¾-inch diameter is drilled into the side of this board at the center line, just one inch above the bottom edge.

Now a threaded pipe pushed through the hole at the top edge will intersect the larger hole at the bottom. A lock nut is held at the opening while the pipe is turned so the threads catch at the pipe with some clearance for the lamp cord to come

through. Place another lock nut at the top end of the threaded pipe.

The center board can now be set into the center of the box and nailed in place through the sides. The lamp cord is pulled through the pipe and a smooth brass tubing is cut to length so it slips over and covers the threaded pipe. (There is a standard pipe for this purpose.) The lamp socket has a nipple that turns directly on the pipe and is tightened against the smooth tubing.

For the compartment dividers cut three pieces of stock to 2¾-inch width, to fit between the center and the sides. Bore a ⅜-inch hole through one of these to feed wire to the outside (see drawing), and also drill a hole at the side of the mail box so the cord can be taken out of the box. Stagger the positions of these dividers so they can be nailed from both the side and the center. Counterset these and all other nails used in the construction.

The final touch is to round off the edges of the box to improve appearance. •

Left, lamp is especially useful in a study room, can be moved about, hold pencils, erasers, etc.

At the center, drill a hole all the way through for the threaded pipe that holds the lamp socket.

The center board is scribed for top angle cuts and two oval-shaped finger-grip holes are sawn.

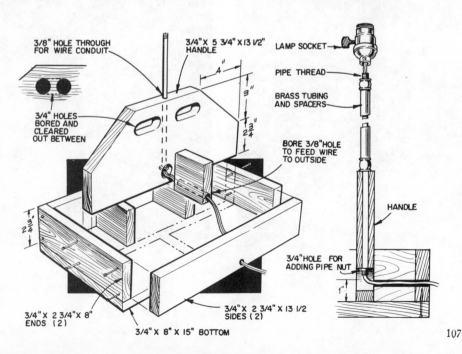

3/8" HOLE THROUGH FOR WIRE CONDUIT

3/4" HOLES BORED AND CLEARED OUT BETWEEN

3/4" X 5 3/4" X 13 1/2" HANDLE

4"

3"

3 3/4"

LAMP SOCKET

PIPE THREAD

BRASS TUBING AND SPACERS

BORE 3/8" HOLE TO FEED WIRE TO OUTSIDE

3 3/4"

HANDLE

3/4" HOLE FOR ADDING PIPE NUT

1"

3/4" X 2 3/4" X 8" ENDS (2)

3/4" X 8" X 15" BOTTOM

3/4" X 2 3/4" X 13 1/2" SIDES (2)

107

Threaded pipe is pushed down, to connect with a hole drilled in side, and is held with lock nut.

A cornering tool and rasp are used to round off all edges and to blend in butt joints at the ends.

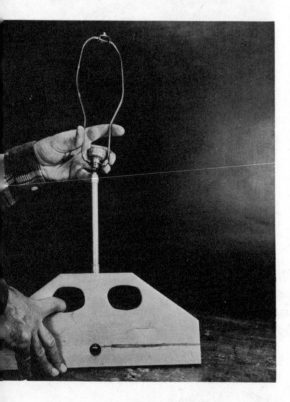

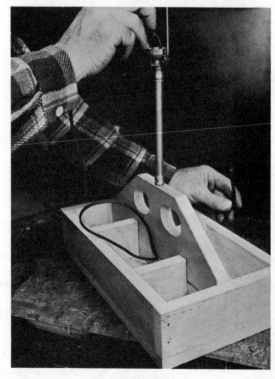

Standard lamp socket has a nipple that turns on threaded pipe; set screw locks on brass tubing.

Electric cord is pushed through to bottom, connects with hole in divider and comes out in back.

Miniature Flower Display

Rich color and design add attractiveness to a spread of natural plants

THE PATINA of natural wood has long been regarded as the natural complement to indoor plants, and pine lends itself particularly to this purpose. Attractive wood planter boxes can be easily finished with penetrating oil stains for deep, rich color. The square design shown in the photos and diagram presents an elegant appearance which is highlighted by a brass ornament. The ornament, in this case, is a standard drawer pull which was popular on cabinets some decades ago and still may be found in the stock of many local hardware dealers.

The planter may be dimensioned to hold any of the standard metal boxes sold at

Stained and polished pine makes ideal containers for flourishing indoor plants. The matching wood boxes are edged with stock contoured moldings and dressed with brass drawer pulls with ornamental design.

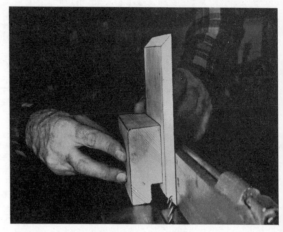

Boards are cut to 4½ inches wide for the sides, 7½ inches long. Ends are mitered at 45 degrees.

The spline slots are cut with the aid of a simple supporting jig made from a small length of 2x4.

Slots are made by leaving blade at 45-degree position with the fence at side close to the blade. Wood glue is brushed into the slots and the wood splines are fitted in. The side pieces are joined by sliding them in position. Bottom panel is then nailed in place and clamp pressure applied against glued corners.

The moldings are cut with rigid backsaw in a miter box. All molding strips must be the same length so the bevels match neatly around the four sides. Slight trimming may be called for. Moldings, at right, are attached at top and bottom with thin brads. Countersink the heads and fill the holes with putty. Sand smoothly before applying penetrating stain.

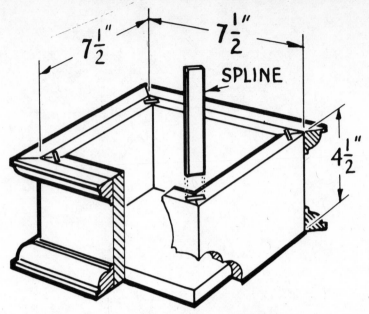

$7\frac{1}{2}''$ $7\frac{1}{2}''$

SPLINE

$4\frac{1}{2}''$

STOCK: $\frac{1}{2}''$ EXCEPT MOLDING

variety stores, though if you're handy with a soldering iron you may want to form your own boxes of thin copper sheeting.

For this project use ½-inch-thick pine or hardwood board, ripped to 4½-inch width, and any type of narrow cove molding. The same molding is used to trim both top and bottom edges, as this tends to make the box look lower and more graceful.

Bevel both ends of each side piece at 45 degrees. The mitered corners will be joined with splines made by ripping narrow strips of the same ½-inch stock. For cutting the spline slots, leave the saw blade at its miter angle, but reverse the position of the fence to the other side. As the board must run through vertically while riding on the thin beveled edge, it will be easier to do this with the aid of a simple jig.

Make the jig from a short piece of 2x4, cutting away an opening on one corner so it will bypass the saw blade. In practice, the piece of 2x4 is held against the thin board to support it while feeding the bevel into the blade, as illustrated. The fence and blade should be set to cut a spline groove about ¼ inch deep into the approximate center of the bevel. Try this out on several pieces of scrap to get it right. Leave the fence and blade setting intact until all eight corners are run through, so the spline grooves will all match perfectly.

Join the sides by brushing glue into the slots and pressing in the spline strips. Get the exact dimension of the bottom opening,

which should be 6½ by 6½ inches, and cut the bottom panel of the same ½-inch board. Nail it into the opening. This will form a square support so you now can apply clamp pressure against the glued corners.

The molding trim, applied along the top and bottom edges, also is mitered at the corners. This is most easily and accurately done with a small backsaw or dovetail saw in a wood miter box. Measure carefully so the four lengths will fit all around. For the amateur, it may be advisable to cut the molding a bit oversize, and trim it down a little at a time as necessary to fit. Use tiny brads or finishing nails for attaching the moldings, and make sure to counterset all nailheads and fill the holes with putty. The brass ornament is attached merely by drilling a hole in the center for a screw which is turned in from the inside of the box.

Finishing of these small pieces is quite interesting. Select an oil stain of a deep, rich color. After the wood is smoothly sanded, apply the stain with a brush or soft cloth. Allow to stand about ten minutes, then wipe off the excess oil and rub the surface vigorously. Follow with another light sanding to remove the raised wood fibers, then seal the surface with a coating of shellac or wax.

If the planters are to stand on a finished table, paste a layer of soft felt on the bottom. •